How To Invest Like A Pro!

Amazing Millionaire Stock Investing Tips Revealed!

You could quickly and easily make a fortune and get filthy rich in this little known, *always on,* "Raging Bull" Stock Market...

Not 1 in 10,000 traders knows this decades proven, iron-clad, counter-intuitive, "**Crash Proof,**" smart money...

Powerful Stock Market *"Raging Bull"* Hot Stock Pick System!

How To *Finally* Beat The Stock Market!

This publication is designed to provide accurate and authoritative information regarding the subject matter covered. It is sold with the understanding that the publisher is not engaged in rendering professional services. If professional advice or other expert assistance is required, the services of a competent professional person should be sought. There is a potential for gain, as well as a risk of loss in Stocks, Forex, Futures, ETF, and Options trading. Securities mentioned herein are presented in an editorial and educational format, and are not being offered as investment or trade recommendations in this book.

All rights reserved. No part of this book may be reproduced in any form or by any electronic or mechanical means, including information storage and retrieval systems, without written permission from the author.

Trademarked names appear throughout this book. Rather than use a trademark symbol with every occurrence of a trademarked name, names are used in an editorial fashion, with no intention of infringement of the respective owner's trademark.

The information in this book is distributed on an "as is" basis, without warranty. Although every precaution has been taken in the preparation of this work, neither the author nor the publisher shall have any liability to any person or entity, with respect to any loss or damage caused or alleged to be caused, directly or indirectly, by the information contained in this book. Information can change. Do your own due diligence.

Copyright © 2015-2016 by Brian Ault. All Rights Reserved.

ISBN-13: 978-1507794920

An iron-clad, *"Crash Proof,"* decades proven *Hot Stock Pick,* "RAGING BULL" Stock Market Trading System for *"Smart Money"* Investors & Traders…

RAGING Bull

Find the FINAL Clues to

$2 MILLION DOLLARS

in GOLD TREASURE

in THIS book!

Hidden, not buried, somewhere in the United States of America…

Consisting of GOLD COINS, GOLD BULLION, ANCIENT HISTORICAL JEWELRY, and PRECIOUS GEM STONES...

"Raging Bull"
Stock Market Trading Contents:

"An investment in knowledge always pays the best interest."
Benjamin Franklin.

Chapter 1 - Page 5: Simple Is Sophisticated

Chapter 2 - Page 8: #1 Hot Stock Pick System!

Chapter 3 - Page 27: Free Hot Stock Pick Software!

Chapter 4 - Page 31: Optional Premium Stock Trading Software

Chapter 5 - Page 39: Top Online Stock Broker Trading Platforms

Chapter 6 - Page 47: IBD – Investor's Business Daily

Chapter 7 - Page 54: Leverage Your Returns Trading Options

Chapter 8 - Page 69: Trade Market Swings With ETF's

Chapter 9 - Page 76: Know When To Buy Hot Stocks

Chapter 10 - Page 85: Know When To Sell Hot Stocks

Chapter 11 - Page 94: IBD's 20 Pro Stock Pick Trading Tips

Chapter 12 - Page 97: Stock Market Trading Plan Outline

Chapter 13 - Page 99: Summary And More Hot Stock Tips

Chapter 14 - Page 113: FREE SPECIAL REPORT! Top 10 Hot Stock And Option Pick Trading Systems And Strategies…
9 Of Which You'll Never Ever Need!

Chapter 15 - Page 137: Free BONUS! Report - Bonus Hot Stock Pick Tips!

Chapter 1: Simple Is Sophisticated

"Things should be made as simple as possible, but not any simpler."
Albert Einstein.

Thank you for your purchase! As promised, you will now learn the single most powerful and profitable trading and investing strategy and hot stock pick trading system available to you today - a must have system for you to survive in the volatile investing arenas we all face today and in this new century. You'll also learn dozens of powerfully proven stock market trading secrets of the pros, including proven championship traders.

Enjoy your new discovery of how you too can pick red hot, money making stocks, as we climb our way to Dow 30,000!

This system strategy is time-tested and proven with real trades and investments made by real traders and investors. It is not hypothetical or based upon theoretical "back-testing."

You don't need to buy a stock or options trading or investing course. You don't need to understand "fundamentals" or "technicals" either (although it helps). It's much easier than all of that complexity, and the software processes all of that information for you anyway.

You won't need overly expensive software or seminars. You won't need books or newsletters or alerts, or the countless dollars and hours needed to buy and read them. You don't have to know "value" or "growth" formulas, or be a math genius either.

Your computer is your best friend, and it can do all the complex calculations for you, and with the simple "point and click" of your mouse, it will quickly and easily pick your new hot stocks for you within seconds.

Doing this the old fashioned way is simply crazy when we have such amazing computing power available to us today. There is simply no need to do complex calculating and charting by hand to select your hot stock picks.

Push the "Easy Button" and let your computer find the golden nuggets for you quickly and efficiently. Your new system strategy will truly be your very own personal **"Secret Stock Market Raging Bull!"**

In the same spirit of thought as Albert Einstein, who coined the phrase, *"Simple Is Sophisticated,"* I will present to you a proven and highly profitable hot stock picking system strategy to have and to employ as your own.

This publication is without fluff and gets directly to the point, and is quickly read, easily understood, and simply employed. It has been stated by high profile publishing companies that a full 90% of all financial and investment books and articles are written by non-investors and non-traders.

This publication is written by a real trader/investor, not a ghost writer, affiliate, or financial writer or economist.

You will confirm and know for yourself that this is a real hot stock picking system and a proven, money winning strategy, employed by real traders *and* investors, complete with examples and real proof.

Most investors are not "day traders." Most investors are "position" traders and investors, being in trade positions from several days, weeks, to several months or years, to give our trades a chance to work themselves out.

It has been found that, unless you're a real day trading pro, the more the average person trades, the more he or she loses from over-trading his or her account.

Day trading is tough, position trading/investing and swing trading/investing is easier.

Also, simply buying and holding (and hoping) is problematic in this new investing era.

We must invest with the stocks and markets in the trending directions and cycles the stocks and markets give to us. This hot stock pick system and strategy will help you to do just that, and to be on the right side of every stock trade.

"As a general rule,
the most successful people in life,
are those who have the best information."
Benjamin Disraeli.

Chapter 2: #1 Hot Stock Pick System

*"Investors operate with limited funds and limited intelligence, they don't need to know everything.
As long as they understand something better than others, <u>they have an edge</u>."*
George Soros, Billionaire Investor/Trader.

Your new hot stock pick system will vastly improve your trading results. Your much improved returns will come to you almost immediately. First, please understand that much of successful trading and investing involves counter-intuition. In other words, sometimes what you think is a good idea, is just the opposite - a very bad idea.

For example, we've all been taught to "buy and hold." In the past, our father's days, maybe this would hold true, most of the time, but not all of the time.

Certainly, in this new age and century, buying and holding (and hoping) without reservation is simply a bad idea, and counter to what you need to know and do going forward in this new investing paradigm of constant and intense change and high volatility.

In the past, events were slower and drawn out over time. Now, events seem to be more intense and more frequent. In the past, you could simply buy and hold almost anything and get away with it (and look brilliant). Now, we do not have the luxury of all boats rising with the longer term rising market tide, because the tide comes and goes much too quickly now, is shorter term, and has a greater volatility.

Instead of being tossed about in an investment dinghy that used to allow you to sit and float long term, we now need to be steering our own power-boat in, out, and around the sea of investment possibilities short, mid, and long term.

To make money in this new era of investing, you must be captain of your own speed-boat, powering your way to and fro and at your will, in order to execute your new hot stock picking system with the intention of making solid and consistent investment returns. Let's go fishing where the real bears and bulls roam…

Your new hot stock picking system consists of the following; a sound and proven strategy that will work for you in bull AND bear markets, and through all seasons and cycles of time (so, you do not need to keep abreast of seasonalities and cycles, unless, of course, you want to).

Your free hot stock pick software and tools will provide you with your "engines," to power your new hot stock picking system through the rough waters of intensely high volatility we all face today.

Your new hot stock pick trading system and strategy can also be applied to your retirement account(s), to bring you the tax-sheltered and compounded returns you want and deserve in these up and down markets.

You may have already seen this stock strategy hiding in plain sight. Maybe you have not seen it. It's a pretty big sea of investment ideas floating around out there. Or, you simply did not recognize it for what it truly is - the single most effective stock picking system available to you today (you don't know what you don't know, until you know it).

Your new hot stock pick trading system and strategy is this; it is simply and effectively screening for stocks that have recently reached their "New 52 Week Highs," and screened on FREE web-based software platforms, with pre-configured and proven stock screeners (see below for all the details). You can easily and quickly pick your hot stocks in minutes a week!

This may seem counter-intuitive to you. You may be thinking, "but, this stock has already made its high, and now it's going to turn and go south." This is generally not true. And this is generally what most people think.

But, we all know that most people (about 90%) don't make money in the stock market. So, in this case especially, you need to think differently than the crowd. This is where most investors and traders get lost. There are so many different stock screens and investment methodologies offered by so many different products and platforms, most folks just don't know where to start or stop, and it can be very confusing.

Now <u>you know</u> what investment strategy to start and end with... <u>new 52 Week High stock picks</u>! Why waste precious time and money with anything else, when this is the best and already decades proven hot stock screening method, strategy, and system on the planet?

You will also have a new confidence in your own stock picking abilities, and you will not have to rely upon gurus, newsletters, or expensive software, that can literally cost you thousands of dollars.

If you do like to be entertained by gurus and newsletters, enjoy them with a renewed confidence in your own stock picking abilities - confirm the good trades, and stay out of the bad trades - and now you can check on them with your own hot stock screen, and **<u>be your own stock market trading guru</u>**! Even if web links and economic conditions change, the "new 52 week high" strategy will still work well, and the "screener" for it will always be found somewhere!

If you're thinking, *"I already know this 52 week high momentum stuff."* Keep reading. It's a bit better than simply "momentum" picks. And, if you already know about it all, why on Earth have you not been trading with it? Open your mind. This is your positive confirmation of what really works. Now profitably trade stocks with it!

A smart investor thinks differently from the crowd. This is why smart investors and traders are labeled as "smart money" in investment circles, and why the average joe is labeled as "dumb money." None of us wants to be labeled as dumb anything, and most of us don't consider ourselves as dumb.

But, where investing and trading stocks and options are concerned, there is a separation of winners and losers that does occur, and it is Darwinian in that, the strong DO survive to trade and invest another day.

So, let's just say we want to invest with smarter money, and to do just that, we need to invest with a winner's strategy - picking stocks that have reached, or are near reaching their 52 week highs! Momentum stocks. Stocks on the move UP. Not just low p/e, or growth, or value screens, etc., but qualified as 52-week high stocks first. Then other qualifiers are gravy.

Let everyone else make their stock selections from the over 100 differing stock screens, and dozens of other stock picking strategies. Let THEM pick the bottom feeding stocks about to turn up – they hope. Let THEM be the dumb money! Change your mind, your thinking, and your investment returns my friend. Think winning, momentum stocks, and stocks reaching their 52 week highs.

These <u>stocks are reaching these new highs for a reason</u> - great fundamentals, which also leads to great technicals (and you don't need to get your Ph.D. in either to benefit from this concept).

And, momentum stocks have been found to continue to be momentum stocks. In other words, a winning stock will continue to be a winner, and for a longer period of time, as compared to other stocks.

AND, stocks reaching new 52 week highs have been researched and found to <u>continue to be winning stocks for even longer periods of time</u>, as compared to stocks picked by other methods or strategies, even in choppy up and down and the most "Bearish" markets.

You don't need to just take my word for it, however. Look at some <u>confirming proof</u> below. You need to be confident in your system strategy, and that it will work for you. <u>It will work for you.</u>

See for yourself...

Your Next Great Stock; How to Screen the Market for Tomorrow's Top Performers, by Jack Hough, on page 152 says, "All things equal, stocks that have gained nicely over the past six months to a year tend to outperform the broad stock market over the next six months to a year. Stocks that are up nicely and are sitting near their 52-week high prices are overwhelmingly more likely to beat the market, and for a longer time."

On page 153 it states, "In 1993, a pair of UCLA finance professors, Narasimhan Jegadeesh and Sheridan Titman, published a landmark paper in the <u>Journal of Finance</u> titled <u>Returns to Buying Winners and Selling Losers: Implications for Stock Market Efficiency</u>. Looking at stock returns between 1965 and 1989, the pair found that stocks that had outperformed the broad market over the past 3 to 12 months tended to continue outperforming it by a margin of a few percentage points per year. But they only maintained that lead for the next 3 to 12 months."

Further, on page 153-155, "In a 2004 study titled, <u>The 52-Week High and Momentum Investing</u>, also published in the <u>Journal of Finance,</u> Thomas George of the University of Houston and Chuan-Yang Hwang of Hong Kong University of Science and Technology set out to crack the code of price momentum. Rather than look for stocks that had merely posted big gains in recent months, as Jegadeesh and Titman had done, they looked for those that were within 5 percent of their 52-week highs."

"The two approaches might sound similar, but there's a critical difference. A stock that has soared over the past year but has dipped in recent weeks might turn up on a search for big gainers, but not on a search for stocks that are near their highs right now. The 52-week-high-method serves to identify stocks with more immediate price momentum. George and Hwang looked at stock prices between 1963 and 2001.... **The 52-week high/low portfolio beat the broad market by 7.8 percentage points a year.** *Remarkably, the returns stayed strong for more than 5 years.*"

"The implications for investors are powerful and specific. **Price momentum matters. The direction that a stock has moved in recent months is more likely than not the direction it will move in coming months.**"

"**That's particularly true of stocks that are making new 52-week highs.**... George and Hwang offered a theory in their paper as to why stocks hitting new highs tend to move even higher. 'Traders appear to use the 52-week high as a reference point against which they evaluate the potential impact of news. When good news has pushed a stock's price near or to a new 52-week high, traders are reluctant to bid the price of the stock higher even if the information warrants it. The information eventually prevails and the price moves up, resulting in a continuation'.... An investor who shies away from a stock hitting new highs does so because he views it as expensive. Ironically, with so many investors thinking the same thing, stocks hitting new highs are often kept less expensive than their growth prospects warrant. That's why you should screen for them."

This is a very good book, and it offers you other screening information as well, including guru screens, which are also discussed below.

Here's more proof, confirmation, and 52 week high stock screening validation for you:

IBD – Investor's Business Daily, uses "stocks at or near 52 week highs" as an important element in its top stocks analysis. IBD boasts Can Slim returns of 1519.18% versus the S&P 500 at 54.9%, from 1998 to June 2007. IBD is discussed at length below, with performance results to 2014, so you can compare pre-2008 results versus post-2008 results. The "L" in Can Slim stands for "Leaders."

More is written about IBD below. IBD's philosophy is this:

- **Quality stocks making new price highs just as they emerge from sound bases on higher volume are often likely to continue climbing, while stocks making new lows are probably headed even lower. Therefore, focus on the new price highs list for the best potential opportunities.**

- **The great paradox of the stock market is that what seems too high and risky to most investors is likely to continue rising. And what seems low and cheap usually goes down.**

- **You can think of a stock's price as a measure of its quality and, consequently, its potential. Typically, stocks higher in price reflect higher quality.**

Millionaire traders/investors Chuck Hughes, John Weston, and Ryan Christopher, all use this 52 week high concept at the core of their investment system. They offer several books on this subject for up to $95, and a $5500 per year newsletter for their top picks, mostly based upon 52 week highs and the use of the 52 week high screen. Chuck Hughes is so confident in this 52 week high system strategy that he promises **an investor could make at least $100,000 per year and up!** He speaks the truth. More on Chuck and John is written in your Free Special Report! area at the end of this publication.

Master Traders, by Fari Hamzei, on page 123, discusses "The company's 52-week highs... Companies make new highs for a reason. A company that is beginning to consistently break new highs may attract new buyers due to the strong underlying fundamentals."

The New Day Trader Advantage, by Jon Markman, inventor of MSN's **StockScouter**, and weekly columnist for MSN Money, as well as a contributor to www.thestreet.com, "working closely with Gradient Analytics, a research and financial engineering firm for institutional money managers, identified statistically predictive traits that affect the performance of successful U.S. securities and developed a systematic way to help discover, research, hold, and sell those securities."

"**StockScouter**, like similar systems that cost Wall Street pros hundreds of thousands of dollars a year, depends on mathematics, software, an innovative mix of measurements... thus, an ideal stock in this system is expected to move briskly and directly to a higher price."

StockScouter, WAS a brilliant "system within a system," and could be used alone to pick the Top 10 or Top 50 hot stocks for you, as well as grade your stock picks from 1 to 10. This online stock picking system screener was discontinued by MSN, and is used here for its quote in support of this books premise of "buy high, sell higher." Funny thing is, MSN HAD a marvelous "52-week highs" screener that they discontinued years ago, BUT they have brought it back! So, I wouldn't be surprised if they bring StockScouter back, or something like it someday. I've included the link to the "52-week highs" screener later.

Jack Carter **(a "former stockbroker, NASDAQ Market Maker, and head trader for a large hedge fund")** sells $3970 software, based upon picking stocks at or near 52 week highs. Mr. Carter writes, **"I discovered that once a stock hit a new 52 week high, it went higher in price 97% of the time."**

Mr. Carter stated further that, "When the stock market experienced its largest point drop in history... Monday, September 17, 2001... the Dow dropped 684.81 points. The Nasdaq dropped 115 points. And yet, as bad as that day was for the overall stock market... 63 stocks actually went up to a new 52 week high! On the Nasdaq, 35 stocks went on to make new highs... the very same day!" (This quote was made prior to DOW -777.68 on 9-29-08.)

His CPA also did an "analysis of the results, which showed that the account was up 286.9% in a 12-month period."

Hot Trading Secrets: How to Get In and Out of the Market with Huge Gains in Any Climate, by J. Christoph Amberger, is a compilation of trading and investing secrets from several traders, investors, and financial writers from Agora Publishing. On page 273, trader/writer Christian DeHaemer writes, ***"Fifty-two-week highs are bullish."***

Entries & Exits: Visits To Sixteen Trading Rooms, by Dr. Alexander Elder, on page 104 states, "First, I look for stocks that have reached a new 52-week high during the past 30 trading days." Worden's TeleChart EasyScans, as well as TradeStation, are also referenced in his book, and are used by many professional investors and traders, and both are discussed below. Dr. Elder and most of his featured investors/traders also use the MACD indicator and moving averages, both of which are also discussed below. The above tools are mentioned here for your early reinforcement of them. Simple is sophisticated.

Just One Thing: Twelve of the World's Best Investors Reveal the ONE Strategy You Can't Overlook, by John Mauldin, on page 20, as written by world renowned investor/trader Dennis Gartman, "Go where the strength is. The objective of what we are after is not to buy low and to sell high, but to buy high and to sell higher."

Dennis is an ex-CBOT trader, who was a frequent guest on CNBC's Fast Money, and he also writes The Gartman Letter, a newsletter for banks, hedge funds, brokerage firms, mutual funds, energy and grain trading companies, and institutional money managers.

Dennis has lectured on capital market creation to central banks and finance ministries around the world, and has taught classes for the Federal Reserve Bank's School for Bank Examiners since the early 1990's.

There are many other stock market books, too many to name them all, like <u>Buy High Sell Higher</u>, <u>Market Wizards, Updated: Interviews With Top Traders</u>, <u>Simple Option Trading Formulas</u>, <u>Getting Started In Chart Patterns</u>, <u>Day Trading For Dummies</u>, <u>24 Essential Lessons for Investment Success</u>, and more, written by experienced investors and traders, that prove 52 week high momentum investing works, and works very well.

A **www.Barchart.com** picture is worth a thousand words…

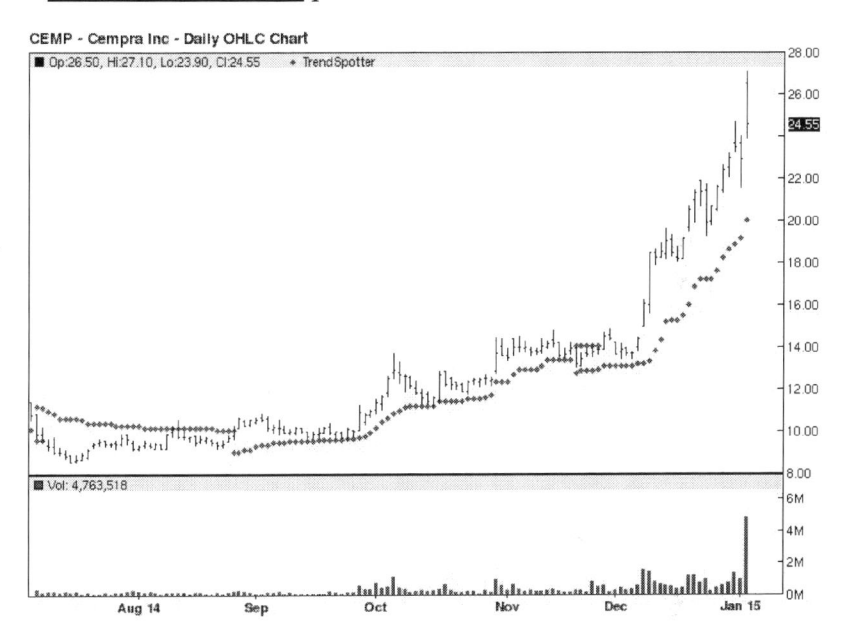

Barchart educational commentary for the above chart is as follows:

"The Chart of the Day is Cempra (CEMP). I found the pharmaceutical company by sorting the **All Time High** list for the stock having the most frequent new highs in the last month. Since the Trend Spotter signaled a buy on 11/26 the stock gained 69.65%."

"Cempra Holdings, LLC is a pharmaceutical company engaged in developing antibiotics for the treatment of bacterial infectious diseases. It focuses on developing antibiotics for treating respiratory tract, skin and skin structure infections and to target the growing problem of antimicrobial resistance."

"Barchart's Opinion trading systems are listed below. Please note that the Barchart Opinion indicators are updated live during the session every 10 minutes and can therefore change during the day as the market fluctuates. The indicator numbers shown below therefore may not match what you see live on the Barchart.com web site when you read this report." The chart and comments are from 1-5-15.

Barchart technical indicators:

- 96% Barchart technical buy signals
- Trend Spotter buy signal
- Above its 20, 50 and 100 day moving averages
- 12 new highs and up 72.50% in the last month
- Relative Strength Index 78.38%
- Barchat computes a technical support level at 20.34
- Recently traded at 24.55 with a 50 day moving average of 16.21

Fundamental factors:

- Market Cap $816.04 million
- Revenue expected to grow 110.30% this year and another 24.5:0% next year
- Earnings estimated to increase 13.40% next year
- Wall Street analysts issued 5 strong buy and 4 buy recommendations on the stock

"The 20-100 Day MACD Oscillator has been the most effective technical trading strategy on this stock and should be used to find an exit point." Barchart as seen above is free.

American Association of Individual Investors (AAII), regularly features stock screening strategies, including screening for stocks hitting new 52 week highs. More on AAII membership is written later.

Even top newsletter editors and traders/writers use 52 week highs in their hot stock pick selection process. I subscribe to dozens of newsletters, so I am not going to mention them all here, just one of my favorites. Richard C. Young's **Intelligence Report**, from InvestorPlace Media, one of the top financial newsletter publishers in the world, in a past newsletter stated, "UL sells its brands in over 100 countries around the world, with over 40% of sales coming from developing and emerging markets. My price chart shows Unilever continuing to make the new 52-week high list. Buy."

It's also included and hiding in plain sight on almost all software trading screens and platforms, paid and free, with the best ones mentioned later. Most good folks just do not recognize the 52 week high screen for its importance and screening power, because there are dozens of other general and lesser screens listed in the same areas, without preference being stated or given to any one specific screen.

And/or most investors simply don't screen at all! Or they don't use the software and computerized tools available to them. They "invest" by using less than reputable means and methods, such as listening to friends and neighbors, or their barber's latest stock tips. Others simply invest by their latest monthly newsletter reco's, which can sometimes be good, but most of the time it is out-dated information, or simply using lesser performing stock selection methods.

Properly screening for your stock picks is imperative in this fast paced, information over-loaded world, to get you the most up-to-date results, to use computer power to scan, screen, search, and select your latest, greatest, hot stock picks.

This is assuming the use of a reliable computer and screening software platform, so you know you can rely upon the data and screening results you obtain. I only discuss proven reliable vendors, to ensure your proper screening results.

<u>If you have not been screening for your stock picks, you are about to start drastically improving your investment results, by the use of smart and proven stock screening strategies for your next hot stock picks!</u>

Additional proof that screening for 52 week high momentum stocks works effectively in up AND down markets follows. Like the entertaining and highly knowledgeable and intelligent Jim Cramer says, ***"There's always a bull market somewhere."***

When the Dow was down <u>-370</u>, I searched for 52 week high stocks, and found the following results...

There were 31 stocks results on MSN; 27 on StockCharts; 24 on BigCharts; 249 at or near highs on Zack's; 49 on optionsXpress; 17 on OmniTrader; 97 on TeleChart with a low p/e high earnings growth rate filter, 73 on TeleChart with an above average earning momentum filter, 270 on TeleChart with an optionable with volume surge filter, and a 158 on TeleChart with a solid dividend yield and dividend growth filter; and 9 on TDAmeritrade's standard 52 week high screen.

Not all of these stock picks are actionable of course, but, as you can see, there are plenty of stocks to research further, correlate, confirm, and select from, <u>even when the Dow is down by almost 400 points</u>!

I later did another search for you, to give you yet another example of a down market still producing good 52 week high results. It's not a fluke. ***You and I can do this on any given market up or down day, and we'll still get good search results.*** The market was again down, this time by <u>-315</u>.

Here are the results: There were exactly 50 stocks on MSN (MSN discontinued their 52 week high screener on 11-2009, and what a shame, but they brought it back); 34 on StockCharts; 38 on BigCharts; 48 on BarChart; 25 on Zack's; 168 on optionsXpress; 654 on all EasyScan TeleChart category screens for 52 week highs; 125 on OmniTrader; and 53 on all 52 week high screens on TDAmeritrade. *There are always more results for you to research further than you'll have money enough to invest in all of them.*

Additionally, many companies found in the first search example, were also found showing up again in the second search example, which is not surprising, and were continuing their run to new 52 week momentum highs. These searches were weeks apart, and many of these same search results will show up weeks and months from now as well.

Lastly, I've researched (and you can too) the 10 worst *"point loss"* days of the DOW, with losses of minus 512.76, -514.45, -554.26, -617.78, -634.76, -678.91, -679.95, -684.81, -733.08, and -777.68 (7%), the biggest point drop in DOW history (back to 1899).

There were literally **DOZENS of 52 week high stocks to trade** on every one of these "bad" days (**25** new 52 week high stocks when -777.68; 1520 lows for the curious).

I was a stock broker and securities analyst in 1987 on the day of the biggest *percentage* point drop in DOW history of **22.6%**!! And yes, there were also plenty of 52 week high stocks worth trading on that day as well. Have some fun, choose *any* trading day and see for yourself.

Let your winners run! **The key is to know where the winners are and how to pick them. This "how do I pick the best stocks" riddle has now been solved for you for your long term trading and investing career success!**

You'll also want to correlate your new 52 Week High hot stock picks with Sector/Industry rotations - which Sectors/Industries are currently performing well, and which Sectors/Industries are not currently performing well. You don't have to do this, but you will increase your odds of picking the best winning stocks from your field of possibilities when you also look for the best performing Sectors/Industries.

You can also get this data from most brokers and premium software platforms, the financial newspaper Investor's Business Daily (IBD), as well as for free on Yahoo at http://biz.yahoo.com/ic/index.html and Google at http://finance.google.com/finance and Financial Visualizations at **www.FinViz.com** under "groups."

It is helpful to know which Sectors/Industries are performing well, because **IBD studies show 37% of a stock's move is directly tied to the performance of the industry the stock is in, and another 12% is due to strength in its overall sector!**

Stock Sectors: Total Returns (%)

Sector Name	5-Day	YTD	1-Month	3-Month	1-Year	3-Year	5-Year
Basic Materials	0.67	-5.17	-3.86	-5.81	-3.98	4.43	2.96
Communication Services	0.85	4.86	-3.17	-1.30	5.67	16.21	12.02
Consumer Cyclical	1.01	2.49	0.31	4.92	3.38	23.51	18.09
Consumer Defensive	1.00	7.87	-0.90	2.84	9.09	15.66	13.51
Energy	0.71	-6.74	-7.97	-14.88	-5.82	3.57	5.48
Financial Services	1.34	9.45	1.93	3.34	10.13	18.47	8.81
Healthcare	-0.74	21.24	-0.88	3.89	22.06	27.04	18.38
Industrials	1.03	7.20	-0.54	2.56	7.95	18.29	14.94
Real Estate	1.17	18.38	-0.28	5.93	18.48	15.61	12.52
Technology	1.52	19.15	0.29	4.35	20.04	22.94	15.41
Utilities	1.78	18.15	0.55	3.02	19.09	11.51	7.01

The above data is as of 1-2-15. Another helpful Industry/Sector link is as follows:
http://news.morningstar.com/stockReturns/CapWtdSectorReturns.html

So, correlate your 52 week high hot stock picks with the currently hot Sectors/Industries, and you'll increase your probabilities of having successful stock picks, as opposed to picking stocks that come from poorly performing Sectors/Industries.

Also, choosing **"best of breed"** stocks in top performing Sectors/Industries, which may not be at 52 week highs at the time, can be an "investing system within a system" on its own, in addition to looking for and selecting 52 week high stocks from sectors, as the two selection methods may or may not offer you the same stock/etf selections at any given time.

Using both methods will correlate and confirm your 52 week high stock picks, as well as offer you additional stock investment candidates – **"the best of the best stocks."**

One of my favorite Warren Buffett quotes is a reinforcement of the above idea - in the context that highly profitable industries can make average money managers seem like geniuses, whereas **industries with poor underlying economics can make even genius money managers seem average or worse.**

Buffett says, *"Managing your career is like **investing - the degree of difficulty does not count. So you can save yourself money and pain by getting on the right train.**"*

Good advice for both investing and career selection. Get on the right money train, and do it the easy way - pick 52 week high stocks - pick hot sectors/industries. In other words, who would you bet on winning a game if playing against each other in ANY game, a proven winner like Michael Jordan, or any "average joe" from anywhere USA? Be a winner - bet on proven winners!

NOTE: Stick with stock picks that are on the NYSE, NASDAQ, and AMEX, that are highly liquid, and that have a minimum price of $15. Stay away from "penny" stocks, even 52 week high penny stocks, or you'll have your account go to zero in record time. Stay away from foreign exchanges - they are not U.S. regulated, and are filled with corruption and manipulation. If you want to invest in foreign companies, do so through U.S. regulated ETF's, mutual funds, and American Depository Receipts – ADR's. Stay away from hedge funds completely.

In sum, picking your hot stocks is a very easy and quick 2 step process - first, **you screen stocks reaching new 52 week highs**, then, you look for the **best performing sectors/industries** that your hot stock picks belong to, match them, and choose the "best of the best" stocks from the "best of the best" sectors/industries, which are connected to your stock picks.

Doing this simple extra step, will increase your probabilities of having more successful and winning stock picks and trade investments. You can use the free and premium software tools below for screening for new 52 week high hot stock picks.

A simplified step-by-step preview and outline of your new hot stock pick trading system; each step is discussed in detail below. It's not difficult, and it doesn't have to be, and now you'll be able to see the whole "Forest *and* the trees:"

1. Screen for hot new 52 week high stocks using FREE stock screeners!

2. Know your hot sectors/industries using Yahoo, IBD, Google, FinViz, or other tools below. http://biz.yahoo.com/ic/index.html and http://finance.google.com/finance and http://news.morningstar.com/stockReturns/CapWtdSectorReturns.html and Financial Visualizations at **www.FinViz.com** under "groups."

3. Select your stock picks. Look at the stock charts. Are they smooth movers, or are they up and down and highly volatile? Choose smooth movers.

4. Is your market favorable for a long bullish trade right now? Is the market bullish or in a bearish pullback? Wait for any *extreme* bearish pullbacks to reverse course, before going long with your bullish stock trades/investments.

5. Execute your selected stock/option trades on your favorite broker platform.

6. Monitor your trade investment positions using your free and/or premium charting software and broker platforms. Most broker platforms also give you running profit and loss totals in your account(s).

7. Exit your trades. Sometimes you'll need to take a loss. Take your profits, and move on to your next trade. See Number 1 and continue your investment process consistently, and over the long term.

Think about these concepts:

* Beginning traders and investors <u>want to know everything</u>, relevant or not, because they do not know the difference.

* Intermediate traders/investors <u>want to apply everything they think they know</u>, which only makes matters more complicated than necessary, which leads to confusion and "analysis paralysis."

* Advanced trading/investing pros <u>know what they need to know</u> - they know what works, and what doesn't, and pros simplify their investing process, because "simple is sophisticated," and sometimes "less is more."

** Even if web links and economic conditions change, *and they will change*, the "new 52 week high" strategy will still work well, and the "screener" for it will always be found somewhere!

Be A Happy Dancing Raging Bull!

Chapter 3: Free Hot Stock Pick Software

"Wide diversification is only required when investors do not understand what they are doing."
Warren Buffett, Billionaire Investor.

I don't know about you, but I just love software, especially FREE software! And the best software, screening tools, and online platform for screening for your 52 week high stock picks (and everything else), is Financial Visualizations at **www.FinViz.com**.

You'll simply love FinViz for all it's free tools and data. It has what you need and want, and more. If you need more, they also offer "Elite" premium services.

MSN also offers you another free "52-week highs" stock screener: **http://www.msn.com/en-us/money/stockscreener/52weekhighs?market=USA**

I have included some screen shots for FinViz, Stock Charts, and Big Charts, for you to see visually where they are and what they look like, to help you find the <u>new 52 week high</u> screens more easily.

They are all easy to navigate and use, and <u>your hot stock screening process will literally only take you a few minutes each day, or once each week, or month, as you prefer it</u>, and as your money allows you to trade more or fewer hot stock candidates.

NOTE: You may also wish to compare and confirm Financial Visualizations www.FinViz.com "New 52-Week High" stock picks with the screeners herein, and other screeners you may have on your personal radar. I am affiliated with www.FinViz.com and Financial Visualizations.

Financial Visualizations

⌄	Sector	Any	⌄	Industry
⌄	Forward P/E	Any	⌄	PEG
⌄	Price/Free Cash Flow	Any	⌄	EPS growth this year
⌄	Sales growth past 5 years	Any	⌄	EPS growth qtr over qtr
⌄	Return on Equity	Any	⌄	Return on Investment
⌄	Debt/Equity	Any	⌄	Gross Margin
⌄	Insider Ownership	Any	⌄	Insider Transactions
⌄	Analyst Recom.	Any	⌄	Option/Short
⌄	Volatility	Any	⌄	RSI (14)
⌄	200-Day Simple Moving Average	Any	⌄	Change
⌄	52-Week High/Low	New High	⌄	Pattern
⌄	Average Volume	Any	⌄	Relative Volume

You may wish to begin by screening for your hot stocks each weekend, in preparation for your trades/investments the following week or month.

I understand there are more screeners out there, for you screening experts, but I have chosen to list only those screeners that I feel are the very best in free screening software, especially in screening for new 52 week highs.

If there is something you are using already and you like it, by all means, continue to use it. And if you are already using the above screens, let this be your confirmation of being on the right investment track.

Chances are high, that this is new material for most of you, and there is much more in the way of new ideas for you below.

You can confirm and correlate your **FinViz** hot stock picks with the following free 52 week high screeners as well. This step is optional, and you don't have to do this, but it helps. **FinViz** picks are reliable, as you will see for yourself over time, if you decide to confirm your stock screen picks with other software tools.

These free stock screeners will give you some of the same hot stock picks, so you can correlate and confirm your **FinViz** picks, and they may also give you additional candidates that may be worth some additional research on your part.

They also offer premium tools if you want what they offer, but this is not necessary.

Remember, Simple IS Sophisticated! I don't like Yahoo's screens, and they do not offer a 52 week high screen. However, I do like Yahoo news and sector/industry information.

www.StockCharts.com and **www.BigCharts.com** also offers you free 52 week high screens. If the links below change, simply use the main url's above, and search for 52 week high screener.

For Stock Charts™ go to: http://stockcharts.com/def/servlet/SC.scan and select the numbered hyperlink for each exchange to see the list of 52 week highs.

www.StockCharts.com

For Big Charts™ go to:
http://bigcharts.marketwatch.com/markets/screener.asp?market=Nyse&report=High52WeekbyPercentGain&x=25&y=20

www.BigCharts.com

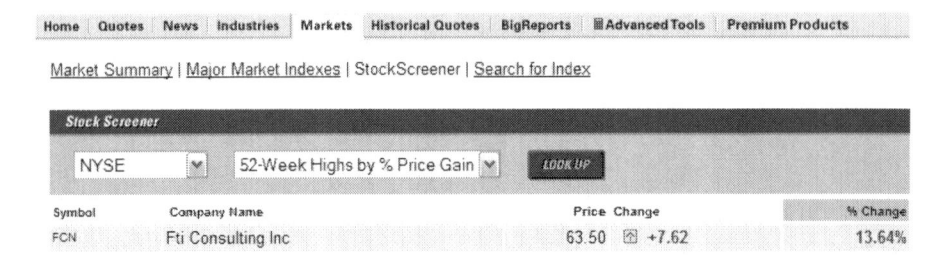

To Review:

1. Pick your **New 52-Week High** stocks.

2. Pick your hot sectors/industries.

3. Pick your hot stocks from the correlated and hottest sectors/industries.

4. Execute your trades.

Chapter 4: Optional Premium Stock Trading Software

"It's not the strongest of the species that survive, nor the most intelligent, but the one most responsive to change."
Charles Darwin, Anthropologist.

Buying premium software is optional. You do not have to buy anything else if you do not want to do so. It depends on how thorough you want to be, and/or how much money you have, and if you like to play with additional software toys like I do.

I must admit, I like to have fun, and trading and investing is definitely fun for me, so I get much enjoyment out of playing with my software. It's always more fun when you win and make money. Otherwise, I'd be doing something else. Hopefully, you will be able to say the same thing sooner than later.

Please note that there exists many premium software packages, and I am aware of this, having researched, demo'ed, and purchased most of them over time. I am simply sharing the best ones with you to keep it simple for you. (Prices may change.)

These products also offer you the lowest cost and best value, in my opinion. You simply do not have to pay thousands of dollars for investment software. Save your money and invest it instead.

I am not a paid affiliate for any of these systems, websites, or products, and I am a paying customer, for the sake of complete disclosure and transparency.

"You adapt, evolve, compete, or die." Paul Tudor Jones II, Hedge Fund Billionaire and trading investor.

TeleChart™ by www.Worden.com offers you good charting and an excellent screen for 52 week highs. TeleChart software is free, and you only pay for the monthly data feed fee ($29.99).

Focus on the <u>Ratings</u> column in your search results, with ratings above 95. You will have plenty of good search results. Your best results will more often than not come from the <u>Optionable Stock</u> selection from the pre-set <u>EasyScans</u>, then under it, select the second selection drop-down area named in the list as ***"Stocks at or near 52 week highs."***

Please refer to the screen shot below. Play with the other <u>EasyScan</u>™ pre-set selections, to compare results and ratings.

Correlate and compare your search results with your FinViz results. Any similar results?

You don't need to pay extra for the Platinum, unless you like to "chat" with other users.

Be careful of listening to others and their varying opinions, because you don't know who you're talking to. (Most web "forums" are simply amateurs with <u>nothing</u> to offer you.)

However, Mr. Worden would be worth chatting with, if you need some coaching.

Telechart by www.Worden.com

Symbol	Company Name	Sort Value
FCN	Fti Consulting Inc	100.00
CPS	Choicepoint Inc	99.81
DBS	PowerShares DB Silver Fund	99.78
CGPI	Collagenex Pharmaceuticl	99.57
CVA	Covanta Holding Corp	99.51
SWC	Stillwater Mining Co	98.32
GDX	Market Vectors Gold Miner...	97.65

Nirvana Systems has **www.OmniTrader.com** ($295) and **www.VisualTrader.com** ($295). OmniTrader offers you great charts, as well as pattern recognition and buy/sell signals for your own selected stocks, as well as for OmniTrader system selected stocks. Look for the pre-configured screens that state New 52 Week High and Stocks At or Near 52 Week High, located in the Focus List.

As with most software packages, OmniTrader™ offers many pre-configured stock screens, and you can play with them, but you simply don't need them all.

VisualTrader is unique in that it offers you visual representations of Industry Sector rotations - which Sectors are currently performing well, and which Sectors are not currently performing well.

You can also get this data from most brokers and premium software platforms, as well as the financial newspaper Investor's Business Daily (IBD), and on Yahoo. Monthly data feed fees are $29.95, and you can get a discount by making just one yearly payment of $299.50.

I repeat the following on purpose - It is helpful to know which Sectors/Industries are performing well, because **studies show 37% of a stock's move is directly tied to the performance of the industry the stock is in, and another 12% is due to strength in its overall sector!**

www.OmniTrader.com

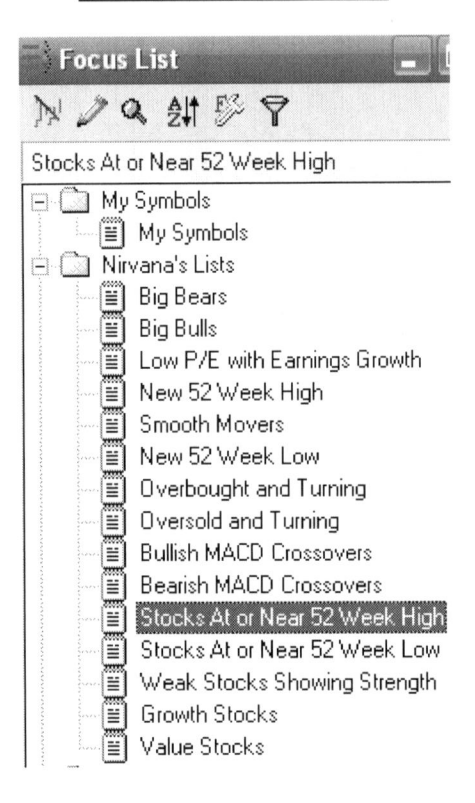

Focus List screenshot showing: Stocks At or Near 52 Week High — My Symbols, Nirvana's Lists (Big Bears, Big Bulls, Low P/E with Earnings Growth, New 52 Week High, Smooth Movers, New 52 Week Low, Overbought and Turning, Oversold and Turning, Bullish MACD Crossovers, Bearish MACD Crossovers, Stocks At or Near 52 Week High, Stocks At or Near 52 Week Low, Weak Stocks Showing Strength, Growth Stocks, Value Stocks).

So, correlate your 52 week high hot stock picks with the currently hot Sectors/Industries, and you'll increase your probabilities of having successful stock picks, as opposed to picking stocks that come from poorly performing Sectors/Industries.

Additionally, both OmniTrader and VisualTrader come in end of day ($295 each) and real-time ($995 each) intraday versions.

Both OmniTrader versions, end of day and real-time intraday, also offer you pre-configured trading patterns and signals recognition, to assist you in your buying and selling decisions and timing. This helps you to take some of the guess-work out of your buy/sell timing.

VisualTrader™ assists you in selecting hot sectors, as well as selecting hot stocks within those top performing sectors.

Both OmniTrader and VisualTrader offer you additional "hot stock picking systems within systems," in addition to the OmniTrader "52 week high screen," and are both worthy of your review and consideration.

American Association of Individual Investors™ at www.AAII.com (only $29/year) offers 50 pre-configured screens from well known gurus and investment methods, such as Peter Lynch, Warren Buffett, Graham, Zweig, value and growth approaches, Weiss, O'Shaughnessy, IBD Stable 70, etc.

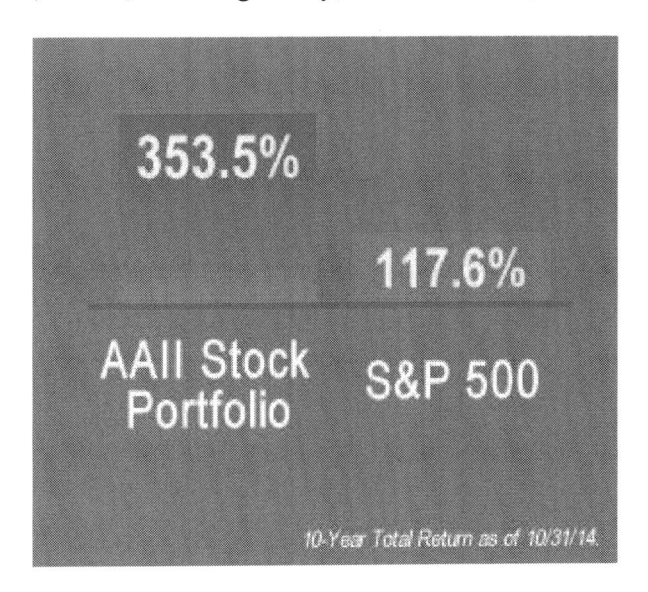

353.5% AAII Stock Portfolio / 117.6% S&P 500
10-Year Total Return as of 10/31/14.

Stock Superstars is a subscription newsletter that gives you their "maximum return at minimum risk" stock picks, at $149 per year, with email buy and sell alerts. *60 well known expert strategies are used to select top stock pick recommendations for you.*

Stock Investor Pro ($198 member price; $247 non-member price) is AAII stock screening software that offers you more and current data, as well as more custom screening features.

AAII has many member benefits, including education, local workshops featuring nationally recognized investment experts, model portfolios, various market data, and a yearly Personal Tax & Financial Planning Guide.

AAII's main 50 screens do not include a labeled "52 week high" screen, but O'Neil's Can Slim screen incorporates this concept in its screen – "L" stands for "Leaders."

Stock Investor Pro™ also has the custom capabilities for screening for 52 week highs.

The importance of the guru screens, for those of you who don't already know, is that these methods have worked well in the past for their namesakes, and the men's names labeling these screens have been highly successful money managers, fund managers, and investors.

Peter Lynch managed the Fidelity Magellan fund. We all know billionaire investor Warren Buffett. Benjamin Graham advocates the value method of investing, and Warren Buffett is a follower of the Graham/Dodd value method, having learned it personally from Ben Graham. As of September 30, 2014, James O'Shaughnessy manages about $7.2 billion dollars in his O'Shaughnessy Asset Management funds.

The O'Shaughnessy screen and investment method is based upon a 52 year study, from 1952 to 2003, based upon data in Standard & Poor's Compustat™ database, and clearly defines the most successful measures in stock investing, and as documented in his book, What Works On Wall Street.

"Even investors who were guided by a quantitative stock selection system can let their human inconsistencies hogtie them." Jim O'Shaughnessy.

So you see, with their screens on AAII, you get to use "their" billion dollar stock investment screening methods for $29 bucks a year! **These screens, in addition to screening for 52 week highs on FinViz, are brilliant, smart, inexpensive, quick, easy, and lazy ways to pick your next hot stocks!**

Equis (Reuters), offers you www.MetaStock.com: $499 end of day, $995 intraday, $59 per month data feed fee, or $595 per year one time payment discount. See their pricing page, as there are *many* other prices and costs to read and understand.

MetaStock™ is a perennial Stocks & Commodities magazine "technical analysis" awards winner for software $500 and up. They offer you 21 "add-on plug-ins" for additional technical analysis, including candlesticks, pivots, chart patterns, etc. These add-ons range in price from $299 to $950, in addition to your main MetaStock software program costs.

TeleChart and OmniTrader are also perennial Stocks & Commodities magazine awards winners. I like OmniTrader better than MetaStock, because OmniTrader is simpler to operate, costs far less, and comes with top "patterns and candlesticks" already built in it with PatternTrader™, and without the additional costs of overly expensive "plug-ins."

Some additional investment tools for reference and fundamental data include; Standard & Poor's 500 Guide (look for other niche S&P guides & books as well); Morningstar Stocks 500; Morningstar ETF's 150; Morningstar Funds 500. Standard & Poor's® and Morningstar® books can be found on www.amazon.com, or at your local Barnes & Noble.

Another surprisingly good book, is the annual The 100 Best Stocks You Can Buy 2015, and for only $14.58 currently on Amazon, it is a very good cross-referencing or stand-alone stock picking tool. It can also be purchased at Barnes & Noble.

There are two drawbacks to books (and monthly magazines and newsletters) - timeliness and strategy - they are static picks, and do not change, no matter what the stocks or markets are doing over time, and the picks are not from your own stock picking strategies or software screening efforts. You must be an avid reader, and truly enjoy *"The Thrill of the Chase."*

NOTE: Prices and offerings may change. Do your own timely research and due diligence.

Chapter 5: Top Online Stock Broker Trading Platforms

*"If I had eight hours to chop down a tree,
I'd spend six sharpening my ax."*
Abraham Lincoln.

There are many broker trading platforms from which to execute your trades. The following are the most high profile, and have the investment tools and screeners that you need and can easily access.

Deep discount brokers, who offer $4.95 trades, don't give you free real-time price quotes, and they're not worth the $5 or $10 dollars saved per trade, in my opinion (customer service is also terrible or non-existent most of the time).

It's more efficient to have real-time quotes to get the most accurate stock and option trades. Trying to save $5 on a trade could cost you hundreds, if not thousands of dollars in the end, because you're getting old and delayed prices, that may be in the wrong direction of your intended trades.

You want to know the accurate prices in real-time, believe me, especially in highly volatile markets. Don't be a cheapskate, because at some point it may cost you dearly if you get the wrong prices from what you intended. In the least case, if you decide to use a delayed quotes discount broker, use "limit orders," where you set the price of your orders.

Most platforms will give you a choice of entering either a "market order," or a "limit order." If you don't specify your order as a limit order, it will be a market order, and you'll get the market price at the time of your order execution, which will be a price you may or may not like.

Retirement accounts, with most brokers, can be opened with no minimums, or with at least $100 to $500 initially.

It's never too late to start saving for your retirement. And you can now get yourself caught up, and you can even get ahead of the retirement pack faster, using your new 52 week high hot stock pick investment system strategy.

I am not a paid affiliate of any of these brokers or trading platforms. I do have accounts with some of them.

www.optionsXpress.com offers you free real-time stock price and option chain price quotes as a standard feature - a must have for current prices and accurate trades. They also offer you market news, research, earnings, stock split info, and a really clean interface.

They have a free screener that is minimal. Look for the 52 week high screen under Price. The results are not as good as FinViz. I like optionsXpress™ for its clean and efficient real-time trade execution.

You also get free online investment seminars. Optionetics™ uses optionsXpress as their underlying broker platform. optionsXpress is a Charles Schwab company.

www.Schwab.com Charles Schwab offers you an excellent and clean online interface, with several pre-defined screens, including a screen for 52 week highs, which brings excellent search results.

They also offer custom screening. Schwab also has an excellent Sector and Industry analysis and performance area, with clear and precise gainers and losers comparisons, including the top-rated stock lists from these sectors/industries for easy viewing.

Schwab also includes, free of charge, stock ratings services from top companies, such as Goldman Sachs, S&P Stars, Argus, and Reuters, as well as top performing etf's and mutual funds.

Schwab™ has good charting for free, including the most important technical and fundamental indicators you need - all in an easy to use format.

Schwab has free real-time quotes, including Canadian quotes, as well as after-hours trading.

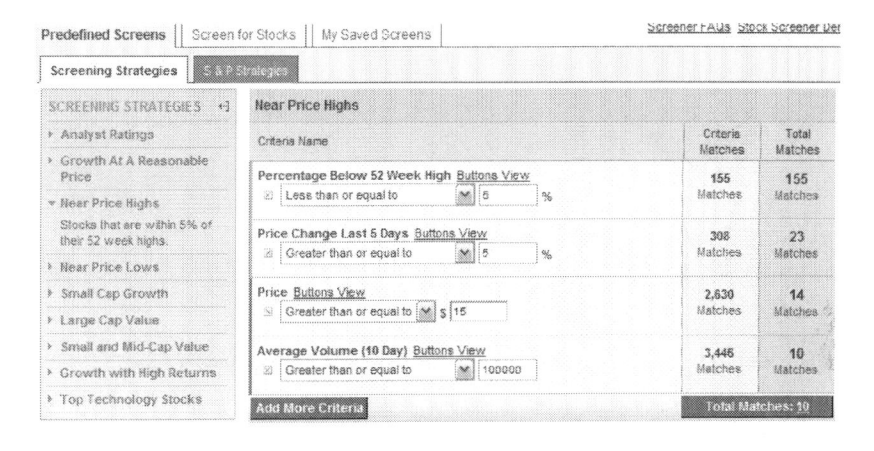

www.Scottrade.com Top choice by J.D. Powers & Associates. Scottrade offers you a basic, custom stock screener, and a pre-set screen for Stocks Approaching their 52 week High. Their alphabetical results include many "penny" stocks you'll want to avoid, so simply click on the Prior Close to invert results to "top down, highest to lowest" prices, to show more tradeable companies.

They also offer basic etf and mutual fund screens, and free S&P Star and Reuter's ratings. Scottrade™ has real-time quotes, with fast execution, and a clean and efficient interface, with free charting and indicators.

I like their sector analysis, and the ability to compare stocks to various sector results, right in the charts as an overlay. Scottrade is a truly cutting-edge trading platform.

They also offer you advanced trading platforms, ScottradeELITE® and Scottrader® Streaming Quotes, but ScottradeELITE® requires a minimum $25,000 balance. Their standard platform is all you really need, and you can open an account with a minimum initial investment of $500. Still just $7 per trade (plus $1.25 per contract for options).

Scottrade is far better than other deep discount brokers that offer $3.95 or $4.95 pricing and delayed quotes.

Scottrade also offers you an options trading platform called OptionsFirst®.

Top Performing Sectors

Transportation	Basic Materials	Financial		Stocks Screener
+0.0%	-0.3%	-15.6%		Create New Screener
YTD Change	YTD Change	YTD Change		Or try one of our Pre-screens:
				High Performing Tech Stocks
Top Performers YTD	Top Performers YTD	Top Performers YTD		0 Criteria Used
Rural/Me... +35%	Converte... +219%			Strong Growth and Value Stocks
Misc. Tran...	Chemical M...	AMT Grou... +4,999,900%		1 Criteria Used
Arkansaa... +30%	Coral Go... +133%	Misc. Fina...		Stocks Approaching their 52 week High
Trucking	Gold & Sil...	Wincroft... +160%		0 Criteria Used
Genesee... +29%	North Am... +107%	Misc. Fina...		High Volume Large & Mega Caps
Railroads	Metal Mini...	Cambrido... +124%		0 Criteria Used
as of 3/7/08	as of 3/7/08	Investment...		Highly Rated Stocks
		as of 3/7/08		0 Criteria Used

www.TDAmeritrade.com offers you real-time stock price and option chain price quotes as a standard feature, news, ratings, research, and sector performance. They offer a free, standard, multiple screener that is pre-configured, and will give you good screen search results for a variety of searches.

They also have a free screener to create "new 52 week high" searches.

Their <u>Advanced Analyzer</u> is free to "Apex" clients, and clients who deposit $100,000 and/or execute at least 5 trades per month. They also offer <u>Trade Architect</u>, and <u>thinkorswim</u> trading platforms, as well as <u>Market Edge</u> news and other trading tools.

TDAmeritrade™ has been very progressive in keeping their trading platform cutting-edge. IBD's <u>Can Slim</u>™ approach to stock selection is a perennial winner, and can be found as a pre-configured stock screener on www.tdameritrade.com.

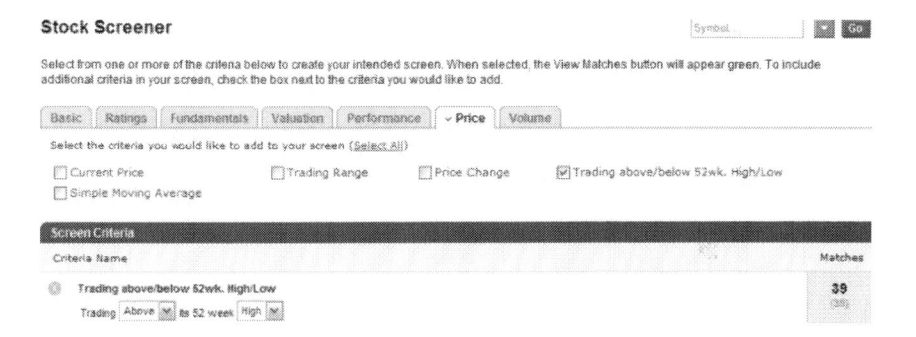

www.TradeStation.com offers you everything and the kitchen sink too. You probably don't need this type of all inclusive platform, unless you are an active day trading professional, who trades stocks, options, futures, and forex.

Free software and web based trading (and a $99.95 per month service fee if trade minimums are not met) will get you every tool, strategy, and indicator that you could possibly want, and far more than you would ever need. It's too complex for most traders.

TradeStation™ is better than Etrade™, in my opinion, if you are willing to pay $99.95 per month for either service, or to meet their trading thresholds for fee waivers.

Visit TradeStation to view their 52 week high tools, and be glad you don't need to worry about all the rest of the listed tools. Trying to know, understand, and implement the rest of the dozens of tools, on any platform, is a big reason for why beginning and intermediate traders and investors are so confused, and don't know where to begin, or what to do next. You don't have to worry about that now!

To see how many confusing tools and indicators exist, visit TradeStation, and be happy you don't need them all.

RadarScreen — Over 180 Technical and Fundamental Indicators

Click on any indicator listed below to view an example and description.

%Chg	Custom Note	Net Percent Change Open	Trade Exchange
%R	Description	Net Change	Trade Size
52-Week Channel	Detrended Price Osc	Net Change Open	Trade Time
52-Week High	Dividends NEW	New 52-wk High	Trades
52-Week Low	DMI	New 52-wk Low	Trades Down

Available Snapshot Information

52 Week High Date	EPS Incl Extra (FY)
52 Week Low Date	EPS Incl Extra (MRQ)
Asset Turnover (AMRQ)	EPS Incl Extra (PTTM)
Asset Turnover (FY)	EPS Incl Extra (TTM)

Hot List Columns

52-Week High	Exchange Traded
52-Week Low	High
Ask	Last
Ask Exchange	Low
Ask Size	Net Change
Beta	News Count
Bid	Open
Bid Exchange	PE Ratio
Bid Size	% Change
Bid Tick	Previous
Category	Shares Outstanding
Date	Symbol
Description	Trade Trend
Dividend	Time
Dividend Yield	Trade Volume
EPS	Trades
Exchange Listed	Volume

www.eTrade.com offers you lots of general bells and whistles (more than you need), world-wide exchange trading, news, research, and real-time price quotes. You must meet minimum trading requirements to qualify for their E*Trade Pro trading platform.

They also have a web based trading platform called E*Trade 360, as well as a mobile trading app.

These plans, especially E*Trade Pro, are for more active traders, i.e. dozens, and even hundreds of trades executed per month.

Etrade has fast trade execution during times of extremely high market volatility. Their screens are ok, but not preferred, and FinViz results are better.

Technicals	
52 Week High	Stock is within [ ] % of its [52 Week High]
52 Week Low	Stock is within [ ] % of its [52 Week Low]
Price closes [Above/Below] exponential moving average (EMA)	[<-20%] [-20 to 0%] [0 to 20%] [20 to 40%] [>40%] Above/Below [13 Day EMA] [50 Day EMA]
13 day EMA is [Above/Below] its 50 day EMA	[Below] [Above]
NEW! Market Edge Picks	[Upgrades] [Downgrades] [Improving] [Deteriorating] [Best Shorts] [Best Longs]

You can also "build your own" mutual funds, etf's, & stocks portfolio(s) with the following: **www.foliofn.com**, **www.fidelity.com**, **www.vanguard.com**, **www.sharebuilder.com**, www.buyandhold.com, www.mystockfund.com.

FolioFn is used by OmniTrader customers for trading directly from their charts ($99 for the plug-in module).

Fidelity™ and Vanguard™ are both premier mutual fund companies, and both also offer stocks, etf's, and options trading.

Sharebuilder, an ING Direct company, offers you $4 trading fees with "automatic investing" plans.

Sharebuilder™ also has good Research and Education sections, to assist you with your retirement and tax questions and concerns.

My Stock Fund offers you deep discount pricing with automatic investment plans and "fractional-share investing," starting with as little as $10 and .99 cent trades.

Buy And Hold offers you a Family Investment Guide, as well as an educational Kids & Investing section.

Buy And Hold and My Stock Fund are two good ways to get your young adult children started with their savings plans and "real-world" investment educations at an early age.

NOTE: Trading platforms, trade execution fees, data feeds, add-on modules, offerings, and general pricing can change. Do your own timely research and due diligence.

"I don't have to make my money back the same way I lost it." ($2 Billion!)
T. Boone Pickens.

Chapter 6: IBD – Investor's Business Daily

"90% of people in the stock market, professionals and amateurs alike, simply have not done enough homework."
William J. O'Neil, IBD Founder.

Investor's Business Daily™ at www.investors.com, in my opinion, is the single *"must have"* investing tool for your premium subscription investing arsenal. In the least case, you should consider the Monday print edition, which comes out on the week-ends, and can be purchased at most book stores and news-stands. IBD gives you reliable top ranking stocks based upon Relative Strength, Earnings, and other proprietary IBD selection criteria.

Their Can Slim™ approach to stock selection is a perennial winner, and can be found as a pre-configured stock screener on **www.tdameritrade.com**, **www.aaii.com**.

Simply searching IBD's paper for its stock selections is more than sufficient, as IBD has already done the fundamental and technical homework for their stock picks. IBD online is more expensive than the print version, and is not necessary. I much prefer the print edition.

IBD offers you a free online "IBD University" for stocks and options courses, Lessons on Buying, Lessons on Selling, Lessons on Options, a Financial Dictionary, and a thorough introduction to their Can Slim investment methods at:
http://education.investors.com/Default.aspx (if this changes over time, simply look for a section titled "Education Center" and/or "Online Courses"). This section is well worth reading. Online sections do change often, so you might want to consider a print subscription to IBD.

IBD also offers continuing education through national IBD Events. Look for a workshop in your area at www.IBDEvents.com. These Beginning Strategies for Successful Investing, Intermediate Strategies for Successful Investing, Chart School, and Can Slim Masters Program workshops range in price from $99 to $8995. These courses are not necessary, but are available to you for your continuing education, if you want them.

Can Slim Private Clients is a service that provides personal portfolio management using the Can Slim investment strategy. You need $100,000 minimum to start with them www.canslimpc.com.

IBD elements to look for specifically, in the context of picking high performance stocks and sectors/industries follows. IBD is formatted beautifully, and they make it very easy to scan for winning stocks. It's worth the subscription either online or offline.

Look for the following news print sections in the least case:

NYSE + Nasdaq Stocks On The Move - SmartSelect® Composite Rating.

IBD's 197 Industry Sub-Group Rankings.

Groups Highest % Of Stocks At New High.

Leading Market Indexes.

IBD Industry Themes.

IBD Special Report.

New Highs.

Exchange Traded Funds and the monthly Winners And Losers.

IBD Daily Stock Lists, i.e. Big Cap 20, IBD's Top 200 Composite Stocks, IBD 100, etc. (IBD 100 is the Monday edition - out on weekends - get this one in the least case.)

				52-wk High	Stock & Symbol		Close Price	Chg	Vol% Chg	Vol 1000	P E
42	56	27	A E D	18.8	Dist&Svc	DYS	10.85	+.10	-61	40	1.8 k
65	54	87	B- C D-	24.7	DoleFood	DOL	20.36	+.90	+55	399	2.0
57	70	41	C B C	24.5	DollarGen	DG	14.29	+.25	-69	514	0.8 o
36	43	22	C- B B-	25.8	DollarThty	DTG	11.75	+.20	+3	187	
56	42	70	D+ B D-	25.5	DominonTr	DOM	19.55	+.65	-41	25	18 k
81	86	63	C+ A C-	69.9	DominRes	D	61.12	-.13	+49	1.6m	4.2 o
96	89	83	A B B	33.5	Donaldson	rDCI	31.55	+.35	-31	94	1.0 k
62	18	90	C D B	10.5	DonnaKaran	DK	10.71	+.04	-86	13	
50	34	57	B- C D-	31.0	DonnellyRf	rDNY	25.50	+.67	+2	334	3.8 o
47	31	44	C+ B C	44.9	Dover	DOV	32.95	-.15	+53	1.2m	1.6 o
60	62	56	D B C+	15.0	DoverDowrs	DVD	12.00	-.14	-9	50	1.5 o
43	14	58	D- B B-	39.7	DowChem	DOW	33.25	-.82	-23	2.1m	4.0 o
37	33	36	D+ B D+	64.0	DowJones	DJ	45.00	+.28	+25	490	2.2 o
59	85	28	A B E	61.4	DownySvgs	DSL	35.14	+.54	-52	106	1.0
99	98	97	A A C+	26.0	DrReddys	RDY	24.90	+2.11	+133	557	.. o
43	65	28	E B B-	35.8	DrilQuip	DRQ	17.06	-.09	+44	79	.. o
63	80	49	D- B B-	40.0	DuaneReace	DRD	29.92	+.43	-34	152	.. o
78	93	56	C+ A D	47.4	DukeEnergy	DUK	38.41	+.70	-12	2.5m	2.9 o
84	95	89	B+ .. C	33.9	Dun&Brad	rDNB	31.26	+.25			.. o

Read any and all research with top ranking, market leading, who's who lists for stocks, industries, and sectors. You'll be amazed at how you begin to see the same top performing stocks over and over again, and you'll remember them.

Also look for relevant company and/or ETF articles and research that shed any positives or negatives upon the performance of your particular stock and sector/industry selections. Definitely look at the company charts IBD provides, to select your smooth movers with high IBD Composite Ratings as well.

Do further research on your stock selections. Check your daily, weekly, and monthly charts for confluence (similarity) in trend directions. Make sure your selections are at actionable buy points, and not declining in a bearish pullback (for going long), but have formed a solid base, and are advancing and within reasonable buy price points (within 5% of base), and not so far extended in price and time, as to be over-extended and declining. More on when to buy and sell is discussed below in separate sections.

An IBD study of the greatest stock market winners found that all-star stocks had, on average, outperformed 87% of the market *before* they began their most dramatic price advances. In other words, they were already in leadership positions. This concept is contrary to the popular bargain-hunting mentality, but is based on historical facts.

If you want to find next year's winning stocks, look at the better-performing stocks *today*. <u>Remember, the biggest winning stocks historically have been, on average, in the top 13% of stocks at the time they began their major advances.</u> To help you identify today's leaders, Investor's Business Daily developed the Relative Price Strength Rating, or RS Rating.

This rating compares the price performance of each stock over the last 12 months, with extra emphasis on the three most recent months. Stocks are rated on a scale of 1 to 99, with 99 representing the top 1% in terms of price movement. So an RS Rating of 85 means that stock is outperforming 85% of all stocks in terms of price performance. An RS Rating of 25 means the stock is being outperformed by 75% of the market and should be avoided.

A good starting point for stock selection is identifying the top two or three stocks with the highest RS Rating in an industry group that's leading the overall market. You can find every stock's Relative Price Strength Rating in IBD *SmartSelect*® Corporate Ratings.

HOW'S YOUR PORTFOLIO DOING?

IBD Sector Leaders	23.5%
S&P 500	6.6%

(YTD as of 10/6/2014)

INVESTOR'S BUSINESS DAILY — Check it out now! »

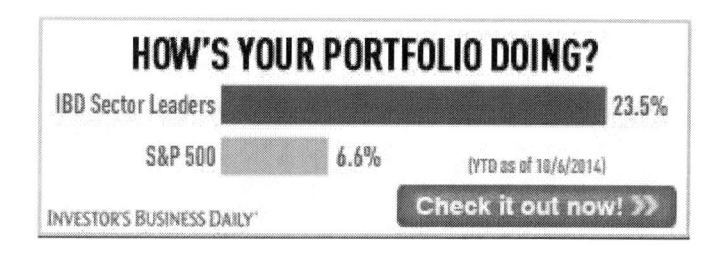

IBD is the single most actionable resource that I've ever seen. If I had one premium resource to choose, it would be IBD. IBD not only gives you relevant securities data, but they show you what it means and how to use it, and they list top stocks, mutual funds, and ETF's in easy to implement lists.

IBD helps you to lower your investment risks, by selecting top performing stocks, mutual funds, and ETF's for you, with their proven successful proprietary investment methods. How easy is that? Pretty darn easy.

Consider a pro's *lazy* way of picking hot stocks, by reviewing IBD's **Leaderboard**.

You'll have more hot stock picks than you'll have money to spend on them.

The American Association of Individual Investors, AAII, reported that "stock performance, from 1998 through to 2007, based upon selecting stocks every month by applying IBD's rules for selecting stocks, was the best among well known growth strategies they analyzed, with a cumulative gain of 1522% versus 55% for the S&P 500 during the same period." (IBD's exact figures are 1519.18% v. 54.9% respectively.)

The Can Slim investment system has also out-performed the S&P 500 through 2014.

Four of the five top fund managers have subscribed to William O'Neil Company's weekly Leaders and Laggards.

Since 1977 this service to top institutional money managers, has averaged 24% per year over the last 30 years, using historically proven investment facts and rules, versus 9.6% per year for the S&P 500.

CAN SLIM® Performance January 1998 - June 2007	
CAN SLIM®	1519.18%
S&P 500	54.9% Source: American Association of Individual Investors

Now let's factor in 2008-2014 results for the below Year To Date (YTD), Five, and Ten Year Returns:

Performance	Passing Companies	Screening Criteria	Chart
	O'Neil's CAN SLIM	S&P 500	
YTD Return:	46.4%	11.9%	
Five Year Return:	9.7%	13.5%	
Ten Year Return:	20.1%	5.8%	
Inception:	25.3%	4.6%	

Data as of 11/28/2014

Lastly, *compare and confirm your FinViz 52 week high picks with IBD picks,* as well as comparing your hot stock picks to any of the other tools you decide to use.

In this way, you add more confidence to yourself and to your hot stock picks, as you compare and confirm your selection tools and their hot stock pick results.

When comparing your separate lists and selections, you'll begin to see the same stocks showing up over and over again, and on different searches and lists.

This *"triangulation"* approach is like using a GPS navigational system, which uses different satellites in different positions, to get a *"fix"* on the desired *"location(s)."*

By using different *hot stock pick* selection tools, you can get a "fix" on certain hot stock picks too. You'll see the best hot stock pick candidates showing up in several "locations."

It really is that easy!

Chapter 7: Leverage Your Returns Trading Options

"Life is really simple, but we insist on making it complicated."
Confucius.

Buying options on stocks and ETF's is a great way to potentially increase and leverage your stock/etf investment returns, by magnifying your stock/etf momentum trends and price swings. (Options can also be traded in the futures markets, but this publication is not about higher risk futures trading.)

Options also allow you to trade both bull and bear markets, up AND down. You can buy "call options" on stocks and/or etf's, if you believe the markets are going up in a bullish fashion. You can buy "put options" on stocks and/or etf's, if you believe the markets are going down in a bearish fashion.

Not all stocks and etf's have options that are tradeable for them. Your software and broker platform tools will tell you which securities are "optionable." You'll then need to look at the individual securities and their corresponding "options chains." These options chains are included on broker platforms who allow options trading.

These options chains will give you the necessary options pricing data you need to know, in order to make and place your options trades. You make or lose money on the movement of the option prices, which are based upon the movement of the underlying securities.

ETF options are similar to options on stocks. Options are contracts to buy (call) or to sell (put) a stock or ETF, at a certain price, on or before a certain date. For deeper protection against loss, investors can also purchase puts on a stock or ETF they hold. This gives investors the opportunity to sell the stock or ETF to the put writer, if it drops below the strike price, locking in the higher price.

ETF options also allow an investor to "trade" the markets in both bull and bear markets, up and down, by trading sector ETF's, as well as by trading "index" bench-marked ETF's like QQQ, DIA, and SPY. Not all ETF's are optionable.

If you decide to trade/invest in options, and your broker approves you for trading options, make sure you understand the **Characteristics And Risks Of Standardized Options**, a copy of which is available from your broker and www.cboe.com. This is a free booklet written by the Options Clearing Corporation (OCC).

The "simple is sophisticated" way to buy bullish call options, in the context of this publication, is this: Pick your 52 week high stocks and/or ETF's first, then buy calls, or write/sell covered call options on them (both are IRA approved), as opposed to buying solely from more complex pricing and volatility methods, calculators, and software screening, using complex strategies.

Buying "cheap," far "out of the money" options, identified from pricing models and newsletters, is what most average traders/investors do. Cheap options are cheap for a reason, and they may just remain cheap when your options expire - gaining you nothing - and losing your money. If you're going to buy cheap, you better know why, and you better know what you are doing, i.e. "I'm going to trade the weekly GDX on the upcoming FOMC Wednesday meeting with a Strangle, with 2 days left to Friday's expiration."

I'm writing a new book on trading weekly options, if options are your "thing." It should be out by the last quarter of 2015 on Amazon. Weekly option trading is exciting, profitable, and risky. This subject needs its own book. For now, keep your options buying centered on the 52 week highs... "buy calls on the way up, and buy "puts" on the way down. Keep it simple.

Think differently here too. Be UN-common. Most investors play options using a pricing method (like Black-Scholes), and/or use expensive options pricing and screener software first. Then the security comes into play secondarily.

Most broker platforms now have free options pricing and screening software that other companies have been selling for up to $1495 to $5000, and with their general and overly expensive options courses too.

Reverse your thinking. Pick your <u>already winning</u> stocks and etf's <u>FIRST</u>, using the 52 week high method - then choose your options pricing from the options chains of your current and underlying 52 week high stock/etf momentum picks. You will find that your investment returns will generally be higher, buying call options on your hot 52 week high stocks, based upon the movement of the underlying stock's price, as opposed to buying calls based solely upon movements in the option prices.

Remember LTCM? <u>Long Term Capital Management</u> was a hedge fund, and in 1998 went bankrupt - using the Black-Scholes, "buy cheap, inefficiently priced options" method. They had lots of money to lose. How much money do you have in comparison? If they didn't make "cheap" work, what makes you think you can make cheap work? Counter-intuitive, isn't it? Yes.

Are options risky? Yes. Are stock and etf investments risky? Yes. Nowadays, is getting out of bed and traveling across town risky? Yes. I don't mean to be flip. But, doing nothing is also risky. Choose your risk wisely. And, don't listen to other people, who have never even bought one options contract, who tell you you're crazy for putting your money into options, simply and only because they are "risky." What do they know? Nothing. And you know more than they do. Don't let average people talk you out of being great.

Like Einstein said, *"Great spirits have always encountered violent opposition from mediocre minds."*

Keep it simple. You do not need to know 40 + options strategies - the same strategies these expensive seminars teach you - most of which are too complex for the average investor anyway. All you really need is one or two simple options strategies.

<u>You may be allowed to trade and invest in options in your retirement account(s)</u>.

Generally, your retirement account will allow you, upon your broker's approval, to buy long "call" options, to buy "put" options, and to write or sell "covered call" options, also known as "buy/writes," because you are buying a stock or etf, and then writing an option on the underlying stock/etf, and collecting a premium.

That's three strategies, and it's simple, and it's all you really need.

"Spreads" and strategies such as straddles, strangles, condors, etc., are for more advanced traders, and are not generally approved for retirement accounts.

You also need many years of experience, a higher knowledge of options, and a higher income/net worth on your application for options approval (something most books and seminars neglect to tell you). These strategies are not for most people, and do not fit into the context of this publication's content, and our 52 week high strategy.

Covered Call Writing/Selling (Long Stock/ETF, Short Calls In Equal Quantity):

The most common strategy is writing calls against a long position in the underlying stock or etf, referred to as "covered call writing." Investors write covered calls primarily for the following reasons:

1. To realize additional return on their underlying stock by earning premium income.

2. To gain some protection (limited to the amount of the premium) from a decline in the stock price.

Covered call writing is considered to be a more conservative strategy than outright stock ownership because the investor's downside risk is slightly offset by the premium he receives for selling the call.

As a covered call writer, you own the underlying stock, but are willing to forsake price increases in excess of the option strike price in return for the premium. You should be prepared to deliver the necessary shares of the underlying stock (if assigned) at any time during the life of the option. Of course, you may cancel your obligation at any time prior to being assigned an exercise notice by executing a closing transaction, that is, buying a call in the same series.

A covered call writer's potential profits and losses are influenced by the strike price of the call he chooses to sell. In all cases, the writer's maximum net gain, i.e. including the gain or loss on the long stock from the date the option was written, will be realized if the stock price is at or above the strike price of the option at expiration or at assignment.

Assuming the stock purchase price is equal to the stock's current price:

1. If he writes an at-the-money call (strike price equal to the current price of the long stock), his maximum net gain is the premium he receives for selling the option.

2. If he writes an in-the-money call (strike price less than the current price of the long stock), his maximum net gain is the premium minus the difference between the stock purchase price and the strike price.

3. If he writes and out-of-the-money call (strike price greater than the current price of the stock), his maximum net gain is the premium plus the difference between the strike price and the stock purchase price should the stock price increase above the strike price.

If the writer is assigned, his profit or loss is determined by the amount of the premium plus the difference, if any, between the strike price and the original stock price. If the stock price rises above the strike price of the option and the writer has his stock called away from him, i.e. is assigned, he forgoes the opportunity to profit from further increases in the stock price.

If, however, the stock price decreases, his potential or loss on the stock position may be substantial; the hedging benefit is limited only to the amount of the premium income received.

More Options Tips:

The following options tips are not meant to be an all-inclusive treatment of options - as above, just more facts and tips you don't normally read about in most books.

I've included some free options course links for your general options education. There is simply no need for you to pay hundreds or thousands of dollars to learn about options.

Options volume may be an indicator of professional stock buying. Large "block" trades and higher than normal options volume on a stock, may indicate interest in a stock by institutional buyers and "smart money" traders. Pros will sometimes buy options before stocks, as there is greater leverage, and the returns are higher. This can be a signal to you to buy the stocks with higher than normal options activity.

Jon and Pete Najarian use their "Heat Seeker™" technology to follow such trading activities. These brothers know what they are doing. In fact, Jon was an ex Chicago Bear linebacker (Mike Singletary took his job), who started with about $400, and ran that up to about $100 million - trading options. Jon was also a Chicago floor (pit) trader, who started his own trading company, and later sold it to Citadel, one of the largest hedge funds in the world. Pete also played pro football, and co-hosted CNBC's Fast Money.

If you listen to anyone on tv, listen to Pete. Jon made an occasional appearance on Fast Money (off air) - listen to him also. Jon also appears on Reuters, Bloomberg, Dow Jones, Fox News, CBS Radio, CBOE-TV, and appears daily on First Business Television, which is broadcast to about 1.8 million daily viewers in about 200 cities.

They can be found at www.optionmonster.com. Jon is also on CBOE-TV at www.cboe.com. More on Jon and Pete is written below in the Free Report area.

Buy "in the money (ITM)" options that have some real intrinsic value, and are not all extrinsic time value. Don't buy "cheap" options just because they are cheap. They're cheap for a reason, and more often than not, they will expire worthless. This is the downfall of most beginning options traders.

Stocks and etf's trade within defineable ranges, more often than not, and option sellers know and rely upon these ranges. In the least case, buy "at the money (ATM)," or slightly "out of the money (OTM)" options. By slightly, I mean one or two "strikes" (prices) out of the money.

Far out of the money options will most likely expire worthless, as they are outside the "standard deviation" ranges of most stocks/etf's generally.

The closer you are to the "atm" and "itm" strike prices, the greater are your probabilities for more successful trades.

Being an option **"seller/writer"** can increase your odds and probabilities of having more successful options trades, due to the above range trading within calculated "standard deviations" and volatility that most securities follow (their own "personality" and data characteristics). Becoming an options writer requires advanced knowledge and skills, and it is not my intention to make this publication an in-depth treatment of options.

There are plenty of books devoted to options. The tips included herein are generally tips not included in most option books. If you are interested in pursuing options "writing," look at www.amazon.com for The Complete Guide To Option Selling, by James Cordier & Michael Gross (**www.optionsellers.com** for their free newsletter), and Option Writing Strategies For Extraordinary Returns, by David Funk.

"Delta" is a measure that can be used in evaluating buying and selling opportunities. Delta is the option's sensitivity to changes in the underlying stock price. It measures the expected price change of the option given a $1 change in the underlying.

Calls have positive deltas and puts have negative deltas. For example, with the stock price of Oracle (ORCL) at $21.48, let's say the ORCL Feb 22.5 call has a delta of .35. If ORCL goes up to $22.48, the option should increase by $0.35.

The delta also gives a measure of the probability that an option will expire in the money. In the above example, the 22.5 call has a 35 percent probability of expiring in the money (based on the assumptions of the Black-Scholes model). But note: This does not give us the probability that the stock price will be above the strike price any time during the options life, only at expiration.

Delta can be used to evaluate alternatives when buying options. At-the-money options have deltas of roughly .50. This is sensible, as statistically they have a 50 percent chance of going up or down. Deep in-the-money options have very high deltas, and can be as high as 1.00, which means that they will essentially trade dollar for dollar with the stock. Some traders use these as stock substitutes, though there are clearly different risks involved.

Delta	Gamma	Rho	Theta	Vega	Strike
1.00	0.00	0.00	0.00	0.00	20.00
1.00	0.00	0.00	0.00	0.00	22.50
1.00	0.00	0.00	0.00	0.00	25.00
0.77	0.06	0.02	-0.02	0.03	27.50
0.73	0.11	0.02	-0.01	0.03	29.00
0.61	0.12	0.02	-0.01	0.04	30.00
0.49	0.13	0.01	-0.01	0.04	31.00
0.31	0.11	0.01	-0.01	0.04	32.50

Deep out-of-the-money options have very low deltas and therefore change very little with a $1 move in the underlying. Factoring in commissions and the bid/ask spread, low delta options may not make a profit even despite large moves in the underlying. Thus we see that comparing the delta to the options price across different strikes is one way of measuring the potential returns on a trade.

TIME ("Theta") decay can be your friend as an options writer/seller, and can be your enemy as an options buyer. "Writers" know what to do to adjust their positions, as this is an advanced trading strategy.

As an options buyer, you need to leave yourself enough time for your trades to work - preferably about 2 to 6 months. Another mistake made by beginning options traders is to buy options with hours, days, or only a few weeks left to expiration. An option's value will generally deteriorate faster in the last month than in the other months.

During times of higher volatility, options can increase or decrease very rapidly at any time, including up to the day of expiration - you may make lots of money, or you may lose it all very quickly.

You'll want to close your long buy positions (buying puts and calls), preferably before the day of expiry, or your broker will "sweep" your account and close your positions for you, and at a complete loss, as options expire worthless (even if you have some monetary value left in them - so close out your positions yourself!).

Look to close out your positions (at a profit hopefully), and within 1-4 months. If your stock/etf is still rising, open another options position on it – don't let your options expire worthless as an options buyer.

Options sellers/writers don't care if your options expire worthless, as they have already collected their premiums on these options.

Watch your option's underlying stocks or etf's, upon which the options are written. Are these securities moving for or against your options positions?

Remember, if your underlying security moves significantly, and you have purchased cheap, far out of the money options, your option's prices may or may not move to profitable pricing levels, and you'll be wondering why not.

Don't buy "cheap" options as a strategy. It's *not* a good bet.

The "Greeks:"

Delta

The amount an option's price will change, for a corresponding one-point change in the price of the underlying security.

Gamma

Gamma is the rate of change of the delta, for a change in the price of the underlying asset.

Theta

Theta is the "time decay" of the options value, as time passes.

Alpha

Alpha is a ratio of Gamma over Theta.

Vega

Vega is the rate of change of the options value, with respect to the 1% change in the volatility.

Rho

Rho is the rate of change of the options value, with respect to the 1% change in interest rate.

Gauge current market sentiment using the **"VIX" and "puts/calls" ratio.** These measures can be found on most broker platforms, as well as in IBD.

Some brokers use the data from www.ivolatility.com. Higher volatility generally brings a lower market, and lower volatility generally brings with it a rising market. See also www.cboe.com for further volatility details.

Four Steps To Options Trading Success:

If you are serious about treating your trading like a business - and you should be, because it is - here are four steps to further your trading success:

1. Select a stock with opportunity - <u>A 52 week high momentum stock.</u> Stock selection is important because the value of an option is determined first and foremost by the price movement of the underlying stock. Options may become temporarily undervalued or overvalued according to the Black Scholes model, but the price of an option at its expiration is determined solely by the price of the underlying stock. Options lose all time value at expiration, and only contain intrinsic value, which is determined by the price of the underlying stock.

Regardless of how much a call option is undervalued at the time of purchase, it will lose all value if the underlying stock closes below the strike price of the call option at expiration. For this reason when purchasing a call option, you want to focus on a stock that will trade as far above the strike price of the call option as possible to produce the largest profit. At the time of purchase, whether an option is undervalued or overvalued according to an option-pricing model, has little bearing on whether or not the trade will be profitable.

2. Select the right strategy. Buy "calls" on your hot stock picks.
The markets move mostly upward over time - the longer term, and buying call options increases your odds of having more winning trades, especially with a buy strategy of buying calls on your 52 week high stock picks.

Buying "naked" puts, and being a "short" market player, decreases your odds of having winning trades – you'll have more losing trades. Being "short" is a tough game to play. Certainly, if you get a "fat pitch" for playing the markets short - take it, and swing away.

Diversification can also be an important part of successful options investing. This is especially true when trading stock options, instead of trading "index" options on a broad-based index or ETF.

A major advantage of option purchases is "truncated risk," whereby your loss is limited to your initial investment, yet your profit is virtually unlimited. Diversification will allow you to use truncated risk to its maximum advantage by investing in several differing stock/etf option trades.

Although some of your positions may be unprofitable, each profitable trade can offset several unprofitable trades. A diversified stock/etf option portfolio can produce a substantial return, even if one-half of all trades result in total losses.

3. Select the right entry price. Buy after your stock/etf purchase investment. Another important element for successful options trading is the use of a mechanical system that gives you clear buy and sell signals, and does not require subjective interpretation or guesswork. I prefer systems that have a long history of profitability in any type of market condition, and also incur little risk - <u>52 week high stock picks.</u>

Emotional decision making is often a trader's worst enemy. Using a mechanical investing system removes this emotional element from investing.

A trading system eliminates "gut feelings," second-guessing, whims, uninformed decision making, and a host of other emotions that are often responsible for traders failing to obtain a consistent and reasonable rate of return on their investments. See also the <u>When To Buy</u> section below.

4. Select the right exit strategy. Sell at a profit, <u>before expiry</u>. Sell with a "stop loss" to prevent further losses. A good trading system + discipline = success. A good trading system can provide traders the discipline necessary to overcome the dual emotional enemies of fear and greed, which prevent traders from making proper decisions.

Mechanical systems remove the pressure of making buy/sell decisions based on "gut feelings," or trying to predict the future. Instead, decisions are governed by a pre-determined set of rules that have historically provided consistent, market-beating returns.

Knowing when to sell is one of the most important components of a successful investing plan, and one of the leading causes of investor failure. A good mechanical investing system provides clear sell instructions with every trade, and eliminates this emotional obstacle to profitable investing. Get out of your options trades before expiry.

<u>**Remember, your options positions are based upon your 52 week high stock/etf picks, in the context of this publication.**</u>

See also the When To Sell section below. I fully realize there also exists "option spread" strategies, but spreads do not fall within the context of this publication.

Free Stocks and Options Resources:

http://biz.yahoo.com/opt/ gives you free options tools, a free Options 101 course, and a free Options Glossary.

www.optionseducation.org The Options Industry Council offers you free options trading course materials, resources, tools, and options investment information. There is simply no need to buy expensive options courses when you can get almost everything here for free, with many tutorials, interactive strategies, and free options tools and calculators.

www.cboe.com Chicago Board Options Exchange. More free options investing information in their Education and Strategies areas.

Also look for the CBOE "DRJ Report" options report with Dr. J, Jon Najarian of www.optionmonster.com, which also has free educational materials and archived webinars. Jon's brother Pete, who also co-hosted CNBC's Fast Money (off air), is Jon's partner. Both of these men are worthy of your attention. I've written more about them on page 131.

CBOE has many other options experts as well.

www.collectedworksbookstore.com A good general resource for real gold treasures. Look for **Thrill of the Chase**, and **too far to walk**, by Forrest Fenn, you'll be glad you did.

www.borntosell.com Offers you a free resource for identifying high yield **covered call** option plays.

www.MSN.com

www.Yahoo.com

www.Reuters.com

www.BarChart.com

www.BigCharts.com

www.Bloomberg.com

www.StockCharts.com

Financial Visualizations at: www.FinViz.com

Chapter 8: Trade Market Swings With ETF's

"There is nothing that is a more certain sign of insanity, than to do the same thing over and over, and expect the results to be different."
Albert Einstein.

What exactly are Exchange Traded Funds?

ETF's are baskets of securities that are traded on exchanges. ETF's are traded throughout the day and offer portfolio exposure to a variety of sectors, regions, and broad-market indexes, and investors can diversify their portfolio holdings by investing in an index, asset class, or sector. The ability to diversify your portfolio may be one of the most compelling reasons to invest in ETF's.

There are hundreds of ETF's traded on U.S. exchanges. ETF's have been gaining popularity ever since they were introduced on the American Stock Exchange, beginning with SPDR's in 1993, and is currently a multi-trillion dollar market. ETF holders are eligible to receive their pro rata share of dividends, if any, accumulated on the stocks held in an ETF, and interest on the bonds held in an ETF, less fees and expenses.

Fidelity Investments pioneered their "Select" Sector funds in the 1980's (hourly traded NAV's), which funds were/are eerily similar to, and a precursor to ETF's (traded like stocks). I thoroughly enjoyed trading these Select funds way back then.

ETF Options

ETF options are similar to options on a stock. Options are contracts to buy (call) or to sell (put) a stock at a certain price on or before a certain date. For deeper protection against loss, investors can purchase puts for an ETF they hold. This gives investors the opportunity to sell the ETF to the put writer if it drops below the strike price.

ETF options also allow an investor to "trade" the markets in both bull and bear markets, up and down, by trading sector ETF's, as well as by trading "index" correlated ETF's like QQQ, DIA, and SPY, using options.

ETF Bench-marks

There are a variety of different ETF's trading on the market today. Some commonly known ETF's are VIPER's, SPDR's, HOLDR's, iShares, Powershares, Rydex, Diamonds (DIA), and NASDAQ "Q's" (QQQ). ETF's track a wide variety of sectors, regions, and broad-market indexes.

Broad-market based indexes include S&P 500 (SPY), DJIA (DIA), Dow Jones U.S. Total Market, Russell 3000, Large, Mid, and Small-Cap Indexes, Fixed Income indexes, and Specialty Indexes, etc.

Hedging Strategies

ETF's can also be used for hedging purposes. Investors might hedge a portfolio when they think the market, or a sector, is due for a correction, but do not want to sell their holdings.

ETF's can also be used to provide exposure to a particular stock when the investor wants to take a tax loss. In that case, the investor could sell the stock and buy an ETF that matches the same sector. When the wash sale period is expired, the investor could purchase the stock and sell the ETF. Any movement incurred in the stock shares should be similar, although not identical, to those of the ETF.

Are ETF's Right for you?

ETF's are great for investors who want to create a diversified portfolio. ETF's cover every broad-market based index, as well as key sectors, and can be viewed by style, like value or growth, and market capitalization of the category holdings.

There are also specialized ETF's that provide exposure to specific industries and market niches, like gold or energy. There are many ETF's to choose from, but an examination of tax benefits, trading flexibility & strategies, and low expenses, are key in determining if ETF's are right for you. ETF's are passively managed, and have low expense ratios and turnover rates.

How to use ETF's in your Portfolio

ETF's can be used as part of both long term and short term investment strategies. Their low expense ratios and high trading flexibility make them attractive replacements for traditional mutual funds. A common use of ETF's is to invest in broad-market indexes.

Using a few well picked ETF's allows you to gain exposure to major equity and fixed income indexes and market sectors at a low-cost and to get a diversified portfolio. You can also use ETF's to fill in the gaps of your core holdings with more specialized ETF's, like individual sectors, or international stocks. Investors can use ETF's to develop a well diversified portfolio that meets their needs and risk tolerance.

You can trade and invest in sectors, currencies, and "go long or short the markets" using ETF's. Some are also optionable, and most can be traded through your broker, and ETF's can be found in most software platforms (some software even lists the underlying securities in the fund). When in doubt, Google ETF, read IBD, or go to **www.xtf.com**.

ETF's can also be used in your IRA - even some options trading, i.e. buying puts and calls, as well as selling covered calls.

ETF's trade in narrower trading ranges generally, as compared to the general trading ranges of most stocks - especially momentum stocks. This means that generally, a stock is going to run up and down further and longer, as compared to an ETF. ETF's like the DIA, SPY, and QQQ are good for short and mid-term range trading because of this phenomenon.

There are hundreds of ETF's, and some of my favorites include the following symbols. Look them up to see what they are, and to find your own favorites. This is the only way for you to learn about them. It's also fun! ETF's offer you directional trading opportunities during times of low and high volatility, in ever changing up and down markets.

The **QQQ (NASDAQ), DIA (DOW),** and **SPY (S&P 500),** are just three of the more popular and highly liquid ETF's for this type of trading - buying the ETF's directly, and/or buying/selling options on them (not all ETF's are optionable). Here are just a few for you to look up. When in doubt for quotes look-up, just go to Yahoo Finance:

QQQ, FXI, IWM, OIH, GDX, SPY, DIA, ILF, EWZ, EEM, XLE, TLT, TIP, DBA, USO, GLD, SLX, QID, ITB, XHB, DIG, DOG, DUG, SLV, SKF, QLD, SSO, SRS, SDS, DXD, DDM, TWM, SKK, MZZ.

ETF's at www.proshares.com also offer you an excellent means for going long or short the Dow, NASDAQ, and S&P 500 markets, as well as many sectors. Their "Ultra" and "UltraShort" funds move 2 to 1 relative to the respective correlated index bench-mark.

Please check their website or your software platform for the latest fund offerings and price quotes for ProShares and other ETF funds. News and valuation involving the U.S. Dollar, whether weak or strong, can be played through the following ETF's. This is not higher risk futures trading or "spot forex" trading.

You may want to avoid spot forex, as there are some disadvantages to you. Namely, the "retail" level "market-makers" are most of the brokers themselves. Meaning, your own forex broker would most likely be trading against you, and is not a true "inter-bank" forex platform. This is an unfair practice. Trader beware.

Before you trade forex, search Amazon for **How To Become A Successful Forex Trader**, and learn forex first.

If you do decide to give forex a try, use a broker that does not have a "dealing desk," like **www.fxcm.com**.

Stick with highly regulated and transparent ETF's, stocks, and options.

You can't trade futures or forex for your retirement accounts either, but you can trade currency ETF's in your retirement accounts.

RYDEX:
Euro Currency Trust (FXE): Strengthens when Euro strengthens and U.S. Dollar weakens.

Mexican Peso Trust (FXM): Mexican Peso.

Australian Dollar Trust (FXA): A good China play, as Australia is a major exporter of natural resources to China, especially metals. The AUD is known as a "commodity" related currency.

British Pound Sterling Trust (FXB): Invests directly in the Great British Pound (GBP), which is positively correlated to the EUR, only the GBP is slightly more volatile.

Canadian Dollar Trust (FXC): The Canadian Dollar is a "commodity" related currency, and is especially related to oil, diamonds, metals, and natural resources.

Swiss Franc Trust (FXF): The "Swissie" is a "safe haven" currency, and money flows to the CHF in times of crisis and uncertainty.

Swedish Krona Trust (FXS): Swedish Krona.

Japanese Yen Trust (FXY): The Japanese Yen is a good "Chinese Yuan revaluation" play. When the Chinese Yuan increases in value, so does the Japanese Yen.

Weakening Dollar Fund (RYWBX): This fund bets the U.S. Dollar will decrease in value, relative to other currencies. If the USD is weakening, this fund is a hedge, and ideally, the fund will increase in value.

Dynamic Strengthening Dollar Fund (RYSBX): This fund bets the USD will increase in value. Invest in this fund when the USD is strengthening. Look for more funds and thorough offerings information on http://guggenheiminvestments.com/products/mutual-funds/product-list.

Barclay's iShares:
iShares does not currently have any currency specific funds at the time of this writing, but they probably will at some future date. However, they do carry an extensive inventory of foreign "index" funds. www.ishares.com.

ProFunds:
Falling Dollar Fund (FDPIX) www.profunds.com: This fund performs well when the USD weakens. This fund is inversely related to the U.S. Dollar Index (USDX). Rising U.S. Dollar Investor (RDPIX): This fund performs well when the USD strengthens. This fund matches the U.S. Dollar Index (USDX).

ETF's at www.proshares.com also offer you an excellent means for going long or short the Dow, NASDAQ, and S&P markets, as well as many sectors. Please check their website or your software platform for the latest fund offerings and price quotes for ProShares and other ETF funds.

QID is "UltraShort" the Q's (NASDAQ), DXD is "UltraShort" the Dow 30, SDS is "UltraShort" the S&P 500, for some examples.

PowerShares:
Deutsche Bank G10 Currency Harvest Fund (DBV) invests in a "basket" of currencies, including; U.S. Dollar, Euro, Yen, Swiss Franc, Great British Pound, Norwegian Krone, Swedish Krona, Canadian Dollar, Australian Dollar, New Zealand Dollar. www.powershares.com.

Merk:
Hard Currency Fund (MERKX): A no-load mutual fund that invests in a basket of hard currencies from countries with strong monetary policies, assembled to protect against the depreciation of the U.S. Dollar, relative to other currencies. www.merkfunds.com.

Prudent Bear:
Prudent Global Income Fund (PSAFX): Offered by David Tice at www.prudentbear.com. This fund invests 70% (subject to variations) of its portfolio in foreign currency treasuries, i.e. Euro, Germany, Norwegian Krone, and a basket of Asian currencies (these holdings may also vary).

Also look at his **BEARX** mutual fund for a bearish stock market outlook.

ETF Trading Tactics: Have You Heard of the Euro Currency Trust?

During the past few years, the U.S. dollar has fallen against most major currencies.

A simple and easy way for individual investors to profit from the continuing fall of our greenback is this: If you think that Europe's unified currency will rise against the dollar, then a good investment for you would be the **Euro Currency Trust (FXE)**.

The FXE is an exchange-traded fund that moves in parallel with the movements of the Euro. So, if the Euro rises, then the FXE rises.

In sum, ETF's can be traded like stocks, and you can "trade sectors," as opposed to mutual fund end of day "NAV's" for closing buy and sell transactions.

ETF management fees are generally lower than mutual funds.

Additionally, ETF's may have better tax treatment than mutual funds, as mutual funds may pass along tax consequences to the investor, from internal stock turn-over, that ETF's may not pass along to investors.

Also, you can trade options on some ETF's, but you can't trade options on mutual funds.

Three additional ETF resources are IBD, **www.Morningstar.com** and **www.xtf.com**.

Chapter 9: Know When To Buy Hot Stocks

"In this game, the market has to keep pitching, but you don't have to swing. You can stand there with the bat on your shoulder for six months, until you get a fat pitch."
Warren Buffett, Billionaire Investor.

1. **Buy new 52 week high stocks from your screening efforts**, and according to your portfolio rotation schedule and investment plan. Buy and sell your winning and losing stocks/etf/options on a monthly, quarterly, 6 month, or 12 month rotation (or longer if it's still a winning position). Keep your winners and let your profits run until they stop or lose momentum. Sell your dogs and under-performers, according to your investment plan schedule, and buy new 52 week high picks to replace them. Buy momentum, strength, and proven winning stocks - avoid or sell losers, weakness, and "buy & hold hopers." It's that simple.

See the chart following for a visual buy entry. Keep in mind also that you may have had this stock show up on your 52 week highs list earlier, at or around $41 to $42, for an earlier buy entry.

52 week high charts are easy to read and visualize. They go UP! They also have some buy "dips."

The "New High Dip"

1) The stock sets a new 52-week high.

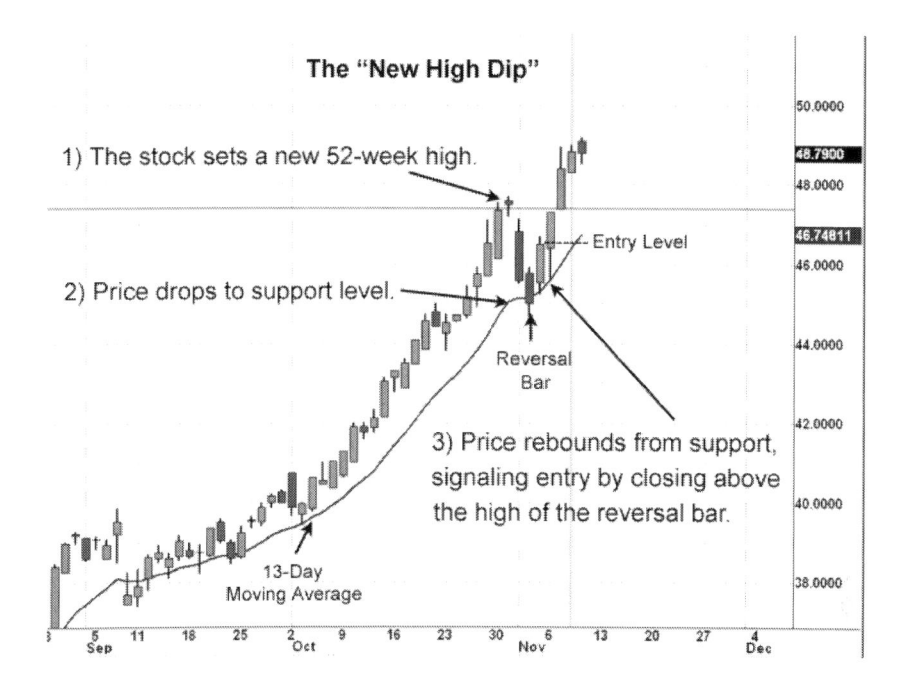

2) Price drops to support level.

Reversal Bar

← Entry Level

3) Price rebounds from support, signaling entry by closing above the high of the reversal bar.

13-Day Moving Average

2. Buy if and when your stock picks are continuing their **upward momentum**, after you have screened for and selected them. Don't buy a stock if it is losing its momentum, is not technically sound and is running out of gas, is reversing from an up-trend to a down-trend, is at the end of its "time" - 6 to 12 months, sometimes 12 months to several years, and is reversing course from an up-trend to a down-trend.

3. **Don't buy if the markets are in _extreme_ 10% to 20% bearish cycle corrections and reversals** (unless you're buying "put" options or "Short" or "UltraShort" ProShares or other "bearish" oriented ETF's or mutual funds). **Wait for the pullback** to run its course - buy on pullbacks in a bullish market, sit on the sidelines in cash or bonds in a bearish market. Being in a "cash" money market or bond position is better than losing your money to a hungry bear market.

The Market Cycle

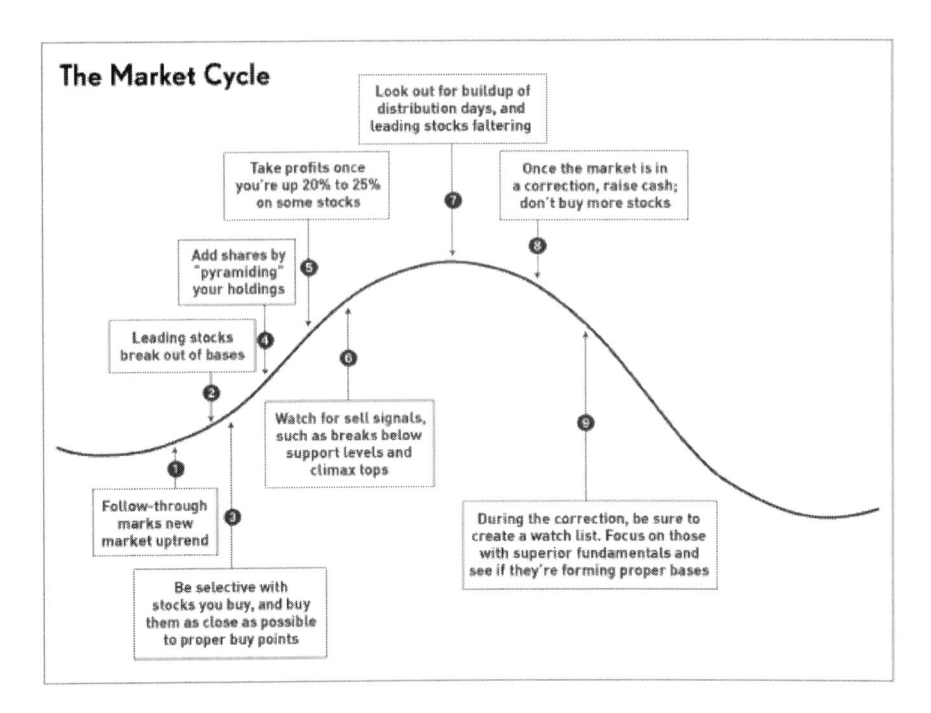

- ① Follow-through marks new market uptrend
- ② Be selective with stocks you buy, and buy them as close as possible to proper buy points
- ③ Leading stocks break out of bases
- ④ Add shares by "pyramiding" your holdings
- ⑤ Watch for sell signals, such as breaks below support levels and climax tops
- ⑥ Take profits once you're up 20% to 25% on some stocks
- ⑦ Look out for buildup of distribution days, and leading stocks faltering
- ⑧ Once the market is in a correction, raise cash; don't buy more stocks
- ⑨ During the correction, be sure to create a watch list. Focus on those with superior fundamentals and see if they're forming proper bases

4. Follow **IBD "buy" guidelines**: as a stand-alone buy method, or as a buy "filter." Make use of their top pick lists, and look at the accompanying IBD stock charts for visual confirmations, and the current standings and ratings of your stock/etf candidates.

See **Your Stock Buying Checklist** below.

Your Stock Buying Checklist

Stock Fundamentals	IBD Research Tables	IBD Mini Charts	Investors.com Stock Research & Stock Checkup	IBD® Charts at investors.com	Market Smith® Premium Charts
Composite Rating 80 or higher	✓	✓	✓		✓
EPS Rating of 80 or more	✓	✓	✓	✓	✓
EPS growth 25% or higher in recent quarters			✓	✓	✓
Accelerating earnings growth			✓	✓	✓
EPS growth past three years 25% or higher			✓	✓	✓
Sales growth 25% or higher in the most recent quarter			✓	✓	✓
ROE 17% or more			✓	✓	✓
SMR® Rating A or B	✓		✓		
Company Star Qualities					
Among the top-rated stocks in its industry group			✓	✓	
New products, service or management			✓		
IPO within the past eight years			✓		✓
Industry Group					
In the top 40-50 groups of IBD's 197 industries		✓			
Industry Group Relative Strength Rating of A or B			✓		✓
In the top six of IBD's 33 sectors					
Industry Demand					
Price above $15 on Nasdaq, $20 on NYSE	✓		✓	✓	✓
Relative Strength Rating 80 or more	✓	✓	✓	✓	✓
Accumulation/Distribution Rating A or B	✓	✓	✓		✓
Increase in number of funds owning the stock			✓		✓
Average daily volume of 300,000 or more		✓	✓	✓	✓
Market Direction					
Market in rally or uptrend			✓	✓	✓
Chart Analysis					
Breaking out of a sound base (cup, flat, etc.)		✓		✓	✓
Volume above-average on breakout		✓		✓	✓
More up weeks than down weeks in the base		✓		✓	✓
Within 5% of buy point		✓		✓	✓
Add shares at pullback to 10-week moving avg. line		✓		✓	✓
Special patterns: 3-weeks tight, etc.		✓		✓	✓
Downward sloping handle in light volume		✓		✓	✓
Relative Strength Line in new high ground				✓	✓
First- or second-stage base				✓	✓

5. Follow your **exponential moving average cross-overs**. Buy short term picks when your 10 period ("Daily") EMA crosses UP over your 20 period EMA on your charts; buy mid-term picks when your 30, or 40 period EMA crosses UP over your 80 period EMA; buy long term picks when your 50 period EMA crosses UP over your 100 or 200 period EMA.

Exponential Moving Averages (EMA's) reflect stock prices and stock price movement directly and more effectively than any other indicator, even if they are lagging indicators (it's better to be late and right, than to be early and wrong).

These are guidelines only, and you may end up buying and selling short term, when you see a 50 EMA cross a 200 EMA, and you may also end up being invested in a long term trade when the 10 EMA crosses a 20 EMA, and both keep going up, to eventually cross the 50 and 200 EMA's.

A 50 EMA crossing up through a 200 EMA is considered to be a **"Golden Cross."** A 50 EMA crossing down through a 200 EMA is considered to be a **"Death Cross"** (just ask any Enron or WorldCom investor, who went down with their ships – or AIG, or the "Freddie Mac's" who fell on their collective "Fannie Mae's").

Be flexible with your technical and EMA tools. There are no hard and fast rules without compromise. For instance, some investors and software platforms use a "21 EMA," rather than a "20," or a 10/50 cross, or a 40/80 cross.

Some traders like **simple moving averages**, SMA's give equal weight to prices, as opposed to EMA's, which give more weight to more recent prices. You get my point. Play with these averages. See for yourself what you like.

Remember also that different stocks may have a different "personality," and your own custom moving average time period may "cup" bottoms and "cover" tops better than a "standard" moving average of 10, 20, 40, 50, or 200, as the 13 MA does above on page 77.

Also remember **short, mid, and long term investment horizons** play to different EMA's and SMA's, i.e. "Daily" chart 10 and 20 moving averages are relatively short term; 40 and 80 are relatively mid term; and 50 and 200 are relatively long term MA's. You can also use "Weekly" and "Monthly" time periods to check for confluence (similarity) over longer time periods.

More is written on MA's in the Summary section below, and how this concept can help you forecast market direction. Day traders usually use 5 minute, 15 minute, 30 minute, and "hourly" charts for shorter term time periods.

In sum, moving averages are very flexible and helpful to you visually, and there is simply no need for you to have dozens of technical indicators on your screen.

Simple is sophisticated.

6. Follow the pre-configured **MACD** – "Moving Average of Convergence Divergence," which is present on almost all software platforms. Use the standard, pre-set periods, as most investors use the standard settings, and you'll get an accurate representation of the moving average cross-overs for your buy/sell signals. You may reset these settings after much experience, if you want to, and you know what you're doing, and why you're doing it.

Most professional traders and investors use MACD and some form of moving average set-up for their buy and sell signals. (If only those good people, who lost their life savings from the Enron and WorldCom debacles, and the like, would have applied just this one principle, they could have saved most of their life savings and not lost it all.)

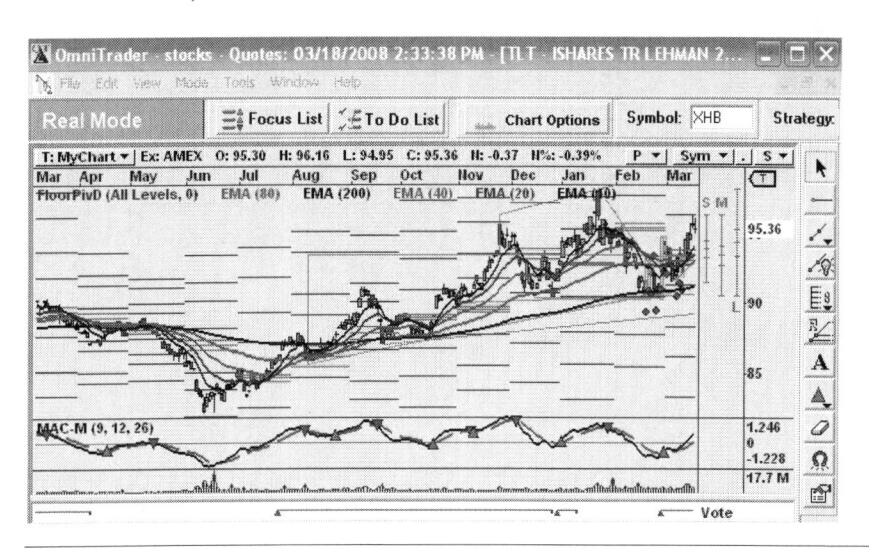

81

7. Follow your buy/sell signals as a filter for your trades/investments, which may be present on your trading software platform(s), i.e. OmniTrader's "Trade Plan," MetaStock, TradeStation, TDAmeritrade's "Trade Triggers," VectorVest, etc.

8. Look at your charts for your stock/etf picks. **Visual images speak volumes**, as to where your stock is positioned along its cycle. Use free charts on FinViz, Bar Chart, MSN, Yahoo, Big Charts, and Stock Charts. Use your premium charts with TeleChart, OmniTrader, TradeStation, MetaStock, and VectorVest. Use your online broker's charts.

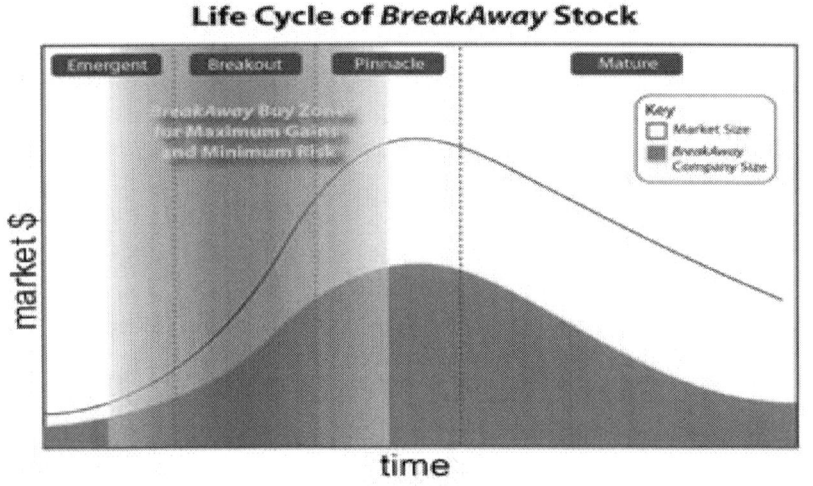

Life Cycle of *BreakAway* Stock

(Chart showing Emergent, Breakout, Pinnacle, and Mature phases with BreakAway Buy Zone for Maximum Gain and Minimum Risk; axes: market $ vs. time; Key: Market Size, BreakAway Company Size)

9. Don't trade just to trade, like a video game, or for the "action." It's better to pass on potential opportunities, than to lose money. There's ALWAYS another trade for another day - far too many for you to trade them all! Be patient. Avoid trading during times of big market declines, due to disasters, or steep corrections (unless you're shorting the market by trading "put" options and/or ProShares™ "Short" or "UltraShort" ETF's, or "bearish" mutual funds).

10. Be careful of stock picks from friends, relatives, and newsletters. Consider the source. And be careful of back-testing and simulated results, as well as books and calendars offering past data and probabilities of what HAS happened in the markets previously during certain calendar days, times, and events. We are in a new and more intense time, and following past data may cause you to lose your money in a big hurry. Things have changed so much that past probabilities from daily calendars just don't work like they used to work. Be careful. <u>Trade the price levels and markets for what they are NOW.</u>

This is not to say that following certain "seasonals" and bullish and bearish "cycles" won't work at all, because they <u>do</u> exist. I'm simply stating that you need to be careful when/if you follow past data and probabilities, because these numbers WON'T add up for you enough times to set you up for <u>too many losing trades</u>. I don't find this kind of data to be actionable any more, for the greater part of the data.

11. In sum, **invest on the side that is winning; go where the strength and momentum are present**; invest like a fundamentalist, and trade like a technician; keep your technical systems and strategies and tools simple; do more of what is working, and less of what is not; don't be afraid to act and to make small mistakes; don't trade with more risk and money than you need to **<u>(1-6% of your money on any one position is proper money management - 10% to 12% per trade is considered higher risk)</u>.**

<u>**Do Not**</u> "dollar cost average your purchases in a down-trend," or throw good money after bad, unless you're adding to winning "short positions" (there is actually one nationally known advocate of dollar cost averaging down – don't listen to her – she's just plain wrong, and was corrected on national TV by a <u>real</u> investment pro – *Ouch!*).

Dollar cost average UP in WINNING positions if you must - buy on "pullbacks" in an up-trend - this is called "scaling in" to your positions - another counter-intuitive maneuver, and a correct one.

The only thing you should be doing in a down-trending stock, is to be considering getting out of it (or "shorting" it), and you can "scale out" of positions, just as you've "scaled in," which is generally done by adding to, or subtracting from, your positions with two or three separate trades, while following your WINNING trend direction.

If you doubt this concept, simply think of Enron and WorldCom to get yourself on the right track, and also remember 2008. "It" *can* and *will* happen again.

12. *"Never let the fear of striking out get in your way."* George Herman "Babe" Ruth.

NOTE: Stick with stock picks that are on the NYSE, NASDAQ, and AMEX, that are highly liquid, and have a minimum price of $15.

Stay away from "penny" stocks, even 52 week high penny stocks, or you'll have your account go to zero in record time, more often than not. Stay away from foreign exchanges, as they are not U.S. regulated, and are filled with corruption and manipulation. Stay away from hedge funds, i.e. the "Bernie Madoffs" of the world.

If you want to invest in foreign companies, do so through U.S. regulated ETF's, mutual funds, and American Depository Receipts – ADR's.

When you can trade new 52 week high stocks that blast off and fly high like rockets, why waste your time and money on anything else like low flying stocks that never get very far off the ground?!

Chapter 10: Know When To Sell Hot Stocks

"When in doubt, punt."
John Heisman.

1. **Sell your losing stocks/etf's/options** on a monthly, quarterly, 6 month, or 12 month portfolio rotation. Keep your winners and let your profits run until they stop or lose momentum, then sell them for a profit. Sell your dogs and under-performers, according to your investment plan schedule, and buy new 52 week high picks to replace them. It's that simple.

2. Sell your stocks/etf's that are **triggering your moving averages and MACD cross-overs from an up-trend to a <u>down-trend</u>**, and have lost their momentum, and their <u>prices are falling BELOW your moving average thresholds</u>, and/or are triggering your stop loss levels.

See more details below concerning stop losses.

See numbers 5 & 6 above in the <u>When To Buy</u> section, and reverse your "cross-over" directions to when your moving averages and MACD indicators move and <u>cross DOWN</u> - opposite of the "buy" indications and instructions above.

"Even when you're on the right track, you'll get run over if you just sit there." Will Rogers.

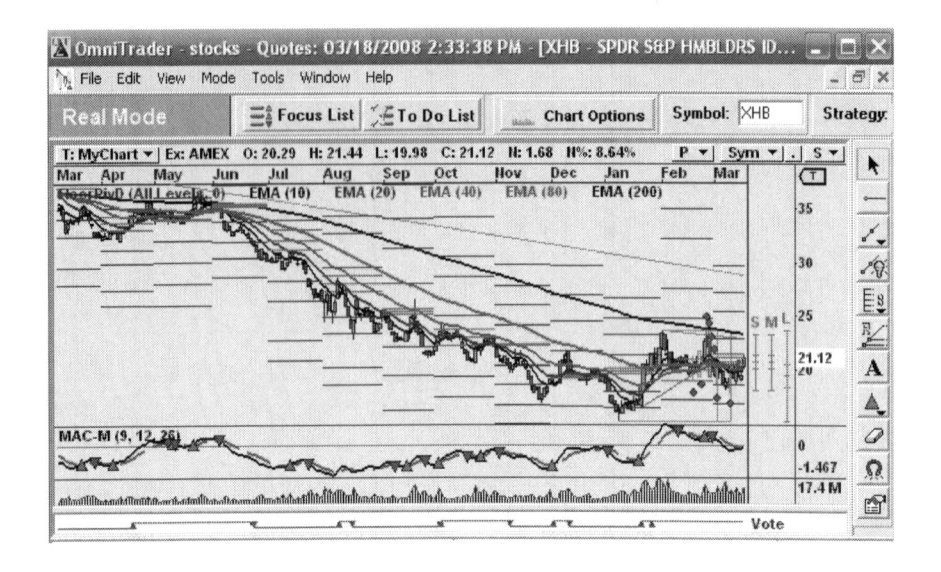

3. **Sell in bearish market cycle corrections and pullbacks that continue in a downtrend, and if your stocks/etf's are following in a down-trend.** If your stops are set at 8% stop-loss levels, this means your stop-loss order is triggered automatically at an 8% loss of equity, even if the market declines to further levels of 10-20% corrections, or more. Stop losses help you to preserve your capital during market pull-backs and *extreme* corrections. (Do *Bears* eat people? Yes! Can a *Bear* eat you? Yes!!)

Some traders, investors, books, and newsletters advocate stops as high as 20-25% stop losses, to allow for wider market fluctuations, without being stopped out of your positions prematurely. IBD recommends an 8% stop loss level. The bottom line is this; how much of your money are you willing to lose on any particular trade investment? This percentage is your monetary ***risk per trade***. (Your *account risk* is "money management.")

Conversely, if you do not use a stop-loss order, your entire dollar amount per trade investment is at risk. The use and management of stop losses and stop loss orders is entirely up to you. **Famous investor Bernard Baruch once said,** *"Even being right three or four times out of 10 should yield a person a fortune if he has the sense to <u>cut his losses quickly</u> on the ventures where he has been wrong."*

4. Follow **IBD** "sell" guidelines as a stand-alone selling method, or as a selling filter. Make use of their top and bottom stock lists, and look at the IBD accompanying stock charts for visual confirmations, and the current standings and ratings of your stocks/etf's.

See **Your Stock Selling Checklist** below.

Your Stock Selling Checklist

✓	Stock Action
	Sell a stock if it falls 8% or more below the price you bought in at
	Consider selling a stock if it climbs 20% to 25% above your purchase price
	*Exception: Hold a stock for at least 8 weeks if it goes up 20% or more within three weeks after its breakout
	Stocks will often flash warning signs on their charts before they fall. Here are some to watch for:
	*New price highs on low volume
	*Falls below 50-day moving average line on the heaviest daily volume in months
	*Heavy-volume sell-off, particularly if the stock experiences the largest price drop of its run
	*Churning: heavy volume and little price progress
	A climax run also signals a stock is near its peak. Here are some signs a stock is undergoing a climax run:
	*Occurs after a long price run up of 18 weeks or more
	*25% to 50% price jump in three weeks or less
	*Largest one-day price gain of its entire run. Daily volume may also be the heaviest of its advance
	*May experience an exhaustion gap, as its price opens significantly higher than the prior day's close
	*Weekly price spread is the largest since the stock began its run

5. Follow your buy/sell signals as a filter for your trades/investments, which may be present on your trading software platform(s), i.e. OmniTrader's "Trade Plan," MetaStock, TradeStation, TDAmeritrade's "Trade Triggers," and VectorVest, etc.

6. Look at your charts for your current stocks/etf holdings. **Visual images speak volumes**, as to where your stock is positioned along its cycle. Use free charts on FinViz, MSN, Yahoo, Big Charts, Stock Charts, and Bar Chart. Use your premium charts with TeleChart, OmniTrader, TradeStation, MetaStock, and VectorVest. Use your broker's charts.

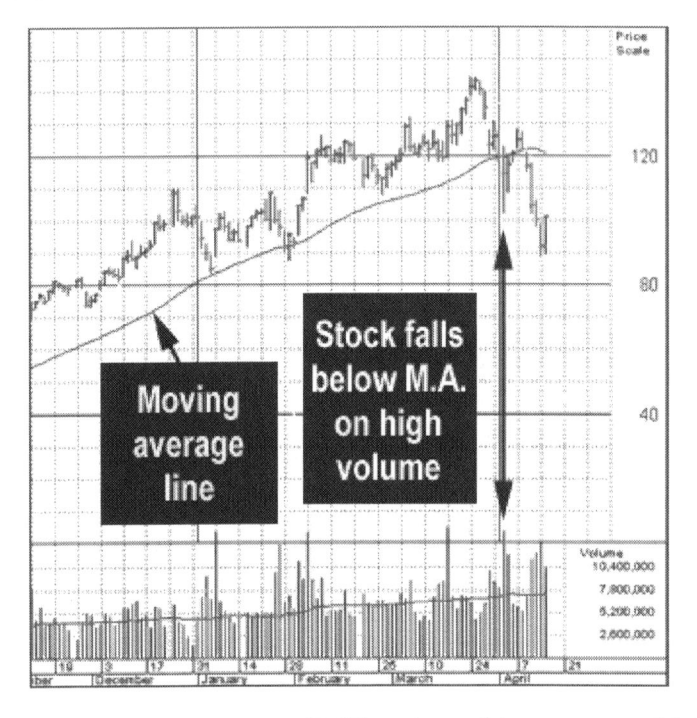

7. **When in doubt, get out - sell.** There's nothing wrong with being in "cash." Be patient. *It is better not to make money than to lose it.*

8. Sell to make money and take your profits! Re-invest your profits. <u>Compound your profits</u>.

Consider compounding your profits further by using a tax-sheltered retirement account. **You can open a retirement account or a regular account, online and in about 15 minutes, with most brokers, if you are a U.S. citizen.**

More Exit Strategies:

Planning your exit is a crucial part of your trading plan, so let's focus on some of the basic methods for getting out of a trade, and a few variables for you to consider.

Traders use a variety of exit strategies. Below I'll discuss a few more of them: Stops; Limit Orders Near Support or Resistance; and Selling at Certain Target Percentage or Dollar Gains. We'll also look at the role that the market environment plays in making your decisions.

Using Stops and Trailing Stops
In most circumstances, the best method to exit a position is to be "stopped out." If we knew when a stock was peaking, it would be better to put in a limit or market order at the peak (or valley) of the price charts.

The reality is, we don't know exactly what will happen tomorrow, so I suggest traders set a stop when they initially enter the position, and then trail it higher as the stock moves ahead ("trailing stop").

Using stops almost always eliminates the chance of a big loss, and at the same time it lets profits run. During times of serious bull runs, this method is great because it works well on stocks that continue to break out.

When the momentum shifts, then traders are stopped out somewhere just below the highs, and they protect their profits and capital, so they can re-enter again when/if the stock begins to move up again.

There are a couple of drawbacks to using stops. First, during choppy times, traders can get stopped out of the trade on intra-day/inter-day volatility, just before the stock moves higher. Second, setting and trailing stops on your stocks takes time, and requires consistent management and review.

Sell Limit Orders Near Support Or Resistance Levels
Sometimes stocks will trade in a range where the support (lower prices in range) is strong at one price level and the resistance (higher prices in range) is strong at another price level. A stock might be in an upward or downward trend and trading in a channel where both the trend line of support and the trend line of resistance look strong.

Some traders enter a long position as the stock bounces up from support and then place a limit order to sell just below the resistance level. This concept is based on the idea that trading within the normal movement of the stock can provide a reduced risk trade profit.

I think this approach is good, but can be improved by using stops and adjusting the "tightness" of the stops, depending on where the stock is located in its channel. For example, after entering the trade and setting the initial stop, I suggest tightening the stop as the stock approaches known resistance levels. Then if the stock moves right through resistance (up-trend), you won't miss the powerful breakout that normally accompanies a break through resistance.

On the other hand, if the stock bounces back down from resistance, you only lose a small amount of your profits. The small downside risk is worth the upside potential, in most cases. If you're "shorting" the market and stock the reverse would be true. You would want to tighten your stops as the stock approaches known support levels.

Selling at a Target Price or Percentage Gain

Some traders watch for a stock to reach a certain target price level before selling. If the stock is at $50, and they believe it will go to $60, they buy the stock and eventually put in a limit order to sell at $60. This approach isn't very time consuming, and for certain types of stocks, it may make sense, but for other types of stocks, it can be a big mistake. Short to mid-term traders tend to use this method.

The downside of the method is that it ignores many of the technical aspects of trading. Furthermore, since most brokers don't allow two sell orders to be in place at one time, traders can't place both a limit order to sell at the target price, and a stop order to protect against a decline.

Traders using this approach need to keep an eye on the stock movement, to know when to change from a limit order to a stop order.

Market Environment

Before planning your exit, look at the market environment. While I recognize that it's impossible to perfectly forecast what the market will do, I do feel that there are times when the general direction of the market appears clear. When the market is choppy, traders may want to lean toward accepting smaller gains, using tighter stops and expecting shorter holding periods.

On the other hand, when the market is hitting on all cylinders, consider looking for bigger gains, using wider stops and generally holding stocks longer.

The market often dictates what types of exit strategies are worth considering, but more often than not, I like the use of setting an initial stop and then trailing the stop higher.

This method is great if the market is consistently pushing stocks to breakout, and works well if stocks are trading in a channel, as traders enter on a bounce off support, and tighten stops near the top of the channel.

Stop Loss Trading Tips:

Setting Stops For Long Positions:

1. Set the stop just under yesterday's low price, unless yesterday was a big up day. Then move the stop closer to today's opening price.

2. Set the stop just under a recent minor support level.

3. Use the daily "Average True Range" to determine the expected movement for the stock, and set the stop slightly below the lower price range.

4. Set the stop the instant your buy order gets filled.

5. Move stops up as the stock rises, first to break even, then to protect profits. On a long position when you use trailing stops, don't lower stops - only raise them.

6. As the stock moves up and tends to "top out," or market conditions become unfavorable, tighten the stop. In other words, move your stop closer to the current market price. Doing this will effectively employ an "up or out" strategy - either the price goes up, or you are out of the trade.

Setting Stops For Short Positions:

1. On daily charts, set the stop just above yesterday's high price unless it was a big down day. Then move the stop closer to today's opening price.

2. Set the stop just above a recent minor resistance level.

3. Use the daily "Average True Range" to determine the expected movement for the stock, and set the stop slightly above the higher price range.

4. Set the stop the instant your order gets filled.

5. Move stops down as the stock declines, first to break even, then to protect profits. When you use trailing stops on a short position, don't raise stops - lower them.

6. As the stock moves down and tends to "bottom out," or market conditions become bullish, tighten the stop, which will effectively employ a "down or out" strategy.

Chapter 11: IBD's 20 Pro Stock Pick Trading Tips

*"The hardest struggle of all,
is to be something different
from what the average man is."*
Charles M. Schwab.

Investor's Business Daily built and studied investing models of the most successful stocks and investors over a 50 year time period. They analyzed all the common characteristics, and what variables occurred before the best stocks had huge advances, and how these variables changed when the stocks reached their top peaks.

1. Consider buying stocks with **each of the last three years earnings up 25%+**, return on equity of 17%+, and recent earnings and sales accelerating.

2. **Recent quarterly earnings and sales should be up 25% or more.**

3. Avoid cheap stocks. **Buy stocks selling at $15 a share and higher.** An IBD study of the best stocks of 1996-97 found that, on average, they made their big jumps when trading at about $25 a share. Only three of the 120 top stocks were trading at less than $10 a share in that period. (*For you "contrarians," see my note below.)

4. Learn how to use charts to spot sound bases and exact buy points. Confine buys to these points as stocks break out on big volume increases.

5. **Cut every loss when it's 8% below your cost.** Make no exceptions, so you can avoid huge, damaging losses. NEVER "average down" in price when buying stocks (don't try to catch a falling knife). This is *risk management per trade*. (Account "Money Management" is *account risk – trade dollar size on any single trade* – "size" matters!)

6. Have selling rules on when to sell and take profits on the way up. A good resource is <u>How To Make Money In Stocks</u>. Look up the section titled, <u>When to Sell and Take a Profit</u>. (See also the <u>When To Sell</u> section above).

7. Buy when market indexes are in an up-trend. Reduce investments and raise cash levels when general market indexes show five or more days of volume distribution (selling off & going lower), as opposed to accumulation (more buying and going higher).

8. Read your preferred financial news to recognize important tops and bottoms in market indexes **(IBD)**.

9. Buy stocks with a **"Relative Price Strength" rating of 85 or higher** in the IBD SmartSelect Composite Ratings. IBD has a proprietary "85-85 Index," that shows <u>the greatest stocks, in every market cycle of the last 50 years, have shown market leading EPS growth and relative price strength, just BEFORE they made their biggest gains</u>! Access IBD's proprietary "85-85 Index" and you can track these stocks in the IBD print edition.

10. Pick companies with management ownership of stock.

11. **Buy mostly in the Top Six broad industry Sectors in IBD's "New Highs" List.**

12. Select stocks with increasing institutional sponsorship in recent quarters.

13. Current quarterly after-tax profit margins should be improving and near their peak.

14. Don't buy because of dividends or P/E ratios. <u>Buy the number one company in an industry, in earnings and sales growth, R.O.E., profit margins, and product quality.</u>

15. Pick companies with a new product or service.

16. Invest mainly in entrepreneurial <u>New America</u> companies (IBD feature). Pay close attention to those with an IPO in the last eight years (not a "new" IPO).

17. Check into companies buying back 5% to 10% of their stock, and those with new management. Research company management and their collective background.

18. Don't try to bottom guess, or buy on the way down. Never "argue" with the market (or try to "push on a string" - let the string [market trend] "pull you" instead). Forget your pride, ego, and emotions.

19. Find out if the market currently favors big-cap or small-cap stocks. **Watch Sector/Industry Group rotation.**

20. Do a post analysis of all your buys and sells. Post on charts where you bought and sold. Evaluate results and develop rules based upon successes and failures. Make adjustments to correct mistakes, learn from your successes and mistakes, and invest accordingly.

* For those of you who enjoy "contrarian" viewpoints, or who simply like to see both sides of the fence, I'm including the following information for you: Jesse Stein has written an interesting book on his similar, but more aggressive view of buying and selling stocks. He's been very successful with his methods. See <u>Insider Buy SuperStocks</u> on Amazon. Most people should diligently follow the above guidelines. Jesse's book is not for the conservative investor.

Chapter 12: Stock Market Trading Plan Outline

*"All our dreams can come true,
if we have the courage to pursue them."*
Walt Disney.

1. **Confirm the general market direction.** Get a big picture view of the Dow, NASDAQ, S&P 500, Russell 2000, indices, etc. Look at any specific market sectors that may interest you – top performing sectors, i.e. technology, energy, transportation, telecom, etc.

2. **Scan for new hot stocks.** Use your **stock screeners**, advisory services, magazines, newspapers, and newsletter services. Where is the big money flowing – both to what stocks, and from what stocks? **Pick your 52 week high momentum stocks!**

3. **Validate and correlate your scanning, screening, and search results.** Do you see similar results showing up in different screening tools?

4. **Confirm your stock selections and their fundamental, technical, and software screening criteria.** Don't trade just to trade. Make sure you have a sound trade and investment.

5. **Execute your trade(s).** Do it accurately and in a timely manner, and with "real-time" quotes.

6. **Check performance on your portfolio and watch list(s).** What are your short and long term results? Check your broker account profit/loss area.

7. **Keep accurate trading records.** Distinguish between short-term "trader" status, and long-term "investor" status. See your tax professional.

8. **Compound your dividends and profits. Don't spend your principal equity.** Know yourself, and why you're doing this in the first and last place.

9. **Shelter your profits in a retirement account. Save.** Compound your profits and reinvest your dividends in a tax sheltered retirement account for the long term.

"I don't know what the seven wonders of the world are, but I do know the eighth – <u>COMPOUND INTEREST</u>." Baron Rothschild.

"Risk is what <u>YOU</u> make of it - choose your risk wisely."

Chapter 13: Summary And More Hot Stock Tips

*"Apply yourself;
get all the education you can,
but then… do something.
Don't just stand there,
<u>make it happen</u>!"*
Lee Iacocca.

Buy stocks hitting <u>New 52 Week Highs</u>! Leverage your investment returns buying call options on your "Hot Stock Picks." Consider "Sector & Industry" strength and rotation, and pick hot stocks in hot sectors and industries.

Buy ETF's for "directional trading," and during times of higher market volatility and "bearish" up and down price swings. Buy "call" and "put" options on ETF's to leverage your returns. Consider the ETF's with symbols DIA, QQQ, and SPY, for directional trading. Also consider the "Ultra" and "UltraShort" ETF's offered by ProShares for "bullish" and "bearish" trading.

Use moving average cross-overs and MACD for your buy and sell signals.

Consider sheltering your compounded returns in an IRA.

Use your favorite software screening, charting, and indicator tools.

Keep it simple.

There were several other chapter subjects I was going to include on cycles, stock splits and buybacks, earnings and all the fundamentals, IPO's, "trading the news," technical indicators, 100's of extra and general resources and links you really don't need, sentiment, and taxes, but, in keeping with our "simple is sophisticated" philosophy, I deleted these sections, as they are simply not needed and not as good as what *is* included.

All you really need is the information that is included herein. The information that I decided to cut out, would have only been a distraction to you, and I saved you about 60 plus pages of reading time and thought, and now you'll have less to remember, and *"less is more"* in this case.

I have encapsulated the ideas generally and simply below, without the background data and calculations and "noise." I am mentioning these ideas, rather than not, so you know them, so you don't waste your time and money on them going forward (unless you want to).

Some services actually center their entire business upon just one of these time-wasting subjects, charging as much as $995 per year for their picks, especially in the subjects of stock splits and IPO's. Save your time and your money.

And of course, Yahoo and MSN also offer free data - **http://biz.yahoo.com/r/** and **http://money.msn.com/investing** including free charts. These charts are not as robust as the premium charts contained herein, or your broker's charts, but Yahoo has upgraded their charts, and they are currently more robust than MSN's charts.

If you want to play with indicators and oscillators; use **Exponential Moving Averages, MACD, RSI, Stochastics. Pivot Points** ("Pro Floor Traders" use Pivots, and they are very similar to support/resistance), and especially **Support and Resistance**, as well as **Trend Lines**.

This publication is not meant to re-hash basics that are repeated everywhere else. You can easily find these indicators and more (too many, and more than you need), as pre-set indicators and oscillators, on most broker and trading software platforms, as well as what they are, and how to use them. Keep your chart indicators as simple as possible.

If you want to further your education in these areas, more power to you. I again suggest, you keep it as simple as possible going forward, and if you want to learn more, stay within the investment principles and guidelines of what is offered to you by Investor's Business Daily (IBD), as IBD falls within our philosophy of picking hot momentum stocks that are high fliers with high relative strength, and are fundamentally and technically sound companies (the "L" in Can Slim stands for "Leaders").

Remember, our 52 week high hot stock pick screening system on www.FinViz.com, as well as AAII and IBD stock selections, and MSN's free "52-week highs" screener, already factor in fundamental and technical analysis for you. What could be easier than that?

Stick with stock picks that are on the NYSE and NASDAQ and AMEX, that are highly liquid, and that have a minimum price of $15. Stay away from "penny" stocks, even 52 week high penny stocks, or you'll have your account go to zero in record time.

Stay away from foreign exchanges - they are not U.S. regulated, and are filled with corruption and manipulation. If you want to invest in foreign companies, do so through U.S. regulated ETF's, mutual funds, and American Depository Receipts – ADR's.

In short, stock splits aren't worth watching or screening for, as they are a rare occurrence, and they may go up as well as down, so they really aren't worth your time. If you do happen to get a stock split in a stock or option that you are invested in already, it may be a signal to you to sell it. Stock splits generally occur after a stock has already made its run to higher prices, and management does a stock split to create a lower priced stock.

Management then hopes that their stock will be seen as an "affordable" value stock - renewing investor interest in their company and stock. Prices may also go up after a split. Be watchful, and be diligent, especially if the stock has already split 2 or 3 times before, which may be a very strong sell signal.

New IPO's used to be worthwhile as a solo trading strategy, and were, for a few stocks, again in 2014, namely Alibaba, but in this new century, new IPO's are fewer, and generally not worth your time as a position trader and investor. Watching for that ONE "Google" or "Facebook" stock is *mostly* a waste of *your* time (it *is* certainly a big pay-day for lucky employees who own stock in such companies, as well as Venture Capitalists). Throw some money into the next hot IPO, when it's available, and see what happens when you trade it, if you *really* want to. Good luck. Paper trading with fake money is always a good idea first.

When you have dozens of hot momentum stock trading opportunities available to you daily, why waste your precious time waiting around for that one "home-run" stock that you may or may not find, or simply reverses course if you do find it?

Certainly, if you DO find one that's worthy, I'm not saying to not invest in it. I'm simply stating the facts - unproven IPO's are currently not what they used to be. Look at the IPO section in IBD on a daily basis, and you'll see what I mean.

Most current IPO's are losers, but there are always exceptions, like the VISA IPO that was up 28% in one day in 2008, and was the largest IPO ever at that time. Now it's **Alibaba Group Holding**, as of this writing on January 5th, 2015. Source: http://www.renaissancecapital.com/IPOHome/Rankings/biggest.aspx

If you feel lucky and smart enough to "trade" these events, by all means do so, but your odds of having *more* winning trades are much higher sticking with your New 52 Week High hot momentum stock strategy, which is a proven, "always on," long-term strategy for *consistent* stock trading profits.

BABA Daily

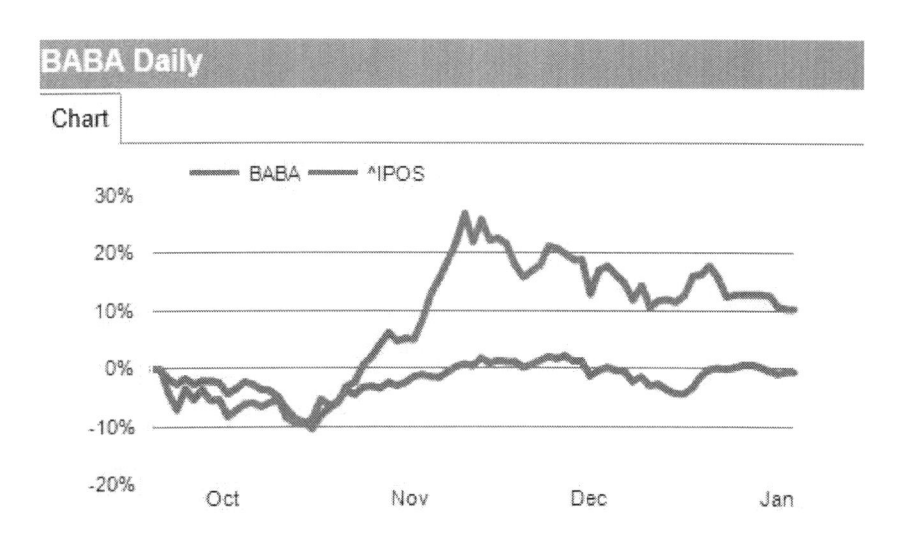

Chart

[Chart showing BABA and ^IPOS percentage change from October through January, with BABA rising to ~25-30% peak in November and settling around 10%, while ^IPOS remains near 0%]

Don't get lost in the "seasonals" and "cycles" in the markets, and the news that goes with them, unless you're trading futures markets. Simply focus on and use your new **"Secret Stock Market Bull Niche"** 52 week high investing strategy to overcome market inefficiencies... there is no better stock screening method or strategy, and it overcomes general market cycles

Keep your eye on the stocks in your portfolio. If you're doing what works, and implementing a winning stock picking system and investment strategy, there is always plenty of time and opportunity for you to use to your advantage.

Use your charting and moving average tools, and follow "Sector Rotation," to keep pace with the ever changing seasons of "bullish" and "bearish" market cycles.

Use your moving averages to buy and sell your stocks during bullish and bearish cycles. Trade prices for what they are now, not what they may be in the future.

Obviously, you need to keep your eyes wide open and use your common sense (which is un-common these days), and sometimes the smartest trade is no trade at all!

If markets are declining, you may wish to stay on the sidelines, in "cash" or money market accounts, or bonds, to preserve your equity, to ride it out, and to wait for the correction to run its full course (unless you are trading "put" options, and/or ProShares Short or UltraShort ETF's, or other "bearish" ETF's or mutual funds).

There is no better measure of investor sentiment than watching the Dow and S&P 500. News will also give you a general positive or negative sense of the markets, but don't get lost in it with "advances/declines," "puts/calls" ratios, etc., unless you are more advanced and you want to, of course. (See "McClellan" below.)

Watch news pertaining to your stock portfolio and the markets generally, but don't try to "trade" the news - leave that to the day traders.

IBD, **http://money.msn.com**, **http://finance.yahoo.com**, and your broker platform news stream, are all you really need to keep current with market news.

"Buy the rumor, sell the news," is a tough game to play, so don't try to trade the news short term. Again, leave *that* game to the day-traders.

Dow 10,000 was thought to be impossible, as we are now approaching Dow 20,000! Do I hear Dow 30,000 coming also? True, the small investors have been mostly sidelined, and we've seen mostly flat to low volumes for a while now, but, with approximately 85% of market moves made by Institutional investors and their BIG money, can you say "market manipulation?" We're being "floated" and the markets are being "propped up" by the FED and the heavy hitters folks. Enjoy the ride, while it lasts. Make YOUR money and know when to run for the sidelines. Get yourself in the game, and know when to get yourself out of the "game." Game, or be gamed.

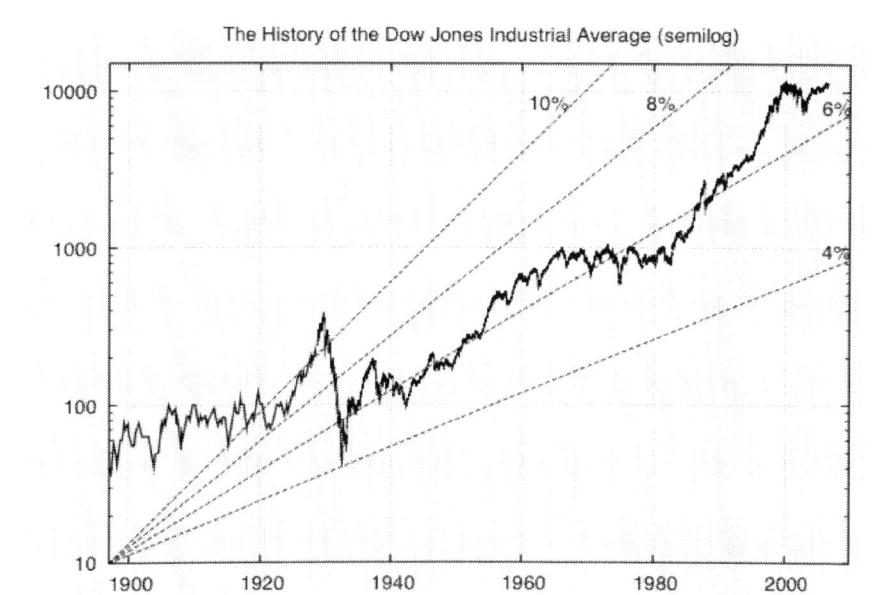

The History of the Dow Jones Industrial Average (semilog)

Invest in your hot momentum stock picks, and "trade" to buy/sell them mid to long term, to capture more profits, and to avoid overtrading your account(s).

Obviously, the news is important, especially when terrorist attacks and disasters cause markets to tumble, and when signaling a general market decline or advance, or during times of governmental intervention. You may wish to remain on the sidelines "in cash positions" during these turbulent times and market conditions.

There has been much governmental intervention starting in 2007, 2008, and 2009, and continuing to 2015, and "Helicopter Ben" and the Federal Reserve have (so far) "dropped" more than $2 TRILLION dollars into "ailing" financial institutions to "help" prop up the economy. It's probably more. What a load of crappola. Our economy is on very thin ice. Where oh where did ALL that money REALLY go!?!? Hint: Foreign and domestic *"banksters."*

Oh my God, Bernanke killed the dollar! You B***d!**

On this type of news, when it was first happening, the Dow raced up +416 points in one day. So if you get a "fat pitch" like this type of news when offered up to you, by all means swing away at it if you want to.

But, be careful with "news event" trading, as the Dow fell a few days later by almost -195 points, then rose again a few days later by +420 on news of the Federal Reserve cutting interest rates yet again, then fell the next day by -293, and then was up the next day by +261! Ad infinitum.

Currently, Janet Yellen's Fed has not raised interest rates (may raise in later 2015), which sent the Dow up another 421+ immediately after the FOMC event in December of 2014. And then the Dow sold off dramatically in December, and today again -331.34 (1-5-15), on continuing news of oil prices dropping to a low of $49.68 per barrel, and settled down $2.65, at $50.04 a barrel, on "large supply without interruption" news by OPEC. America has also become the world leader in energy again. Yeah us! See the Barchart update below for a snapshot on Tuesday morning 1-6-15. Oil's gone even lower.

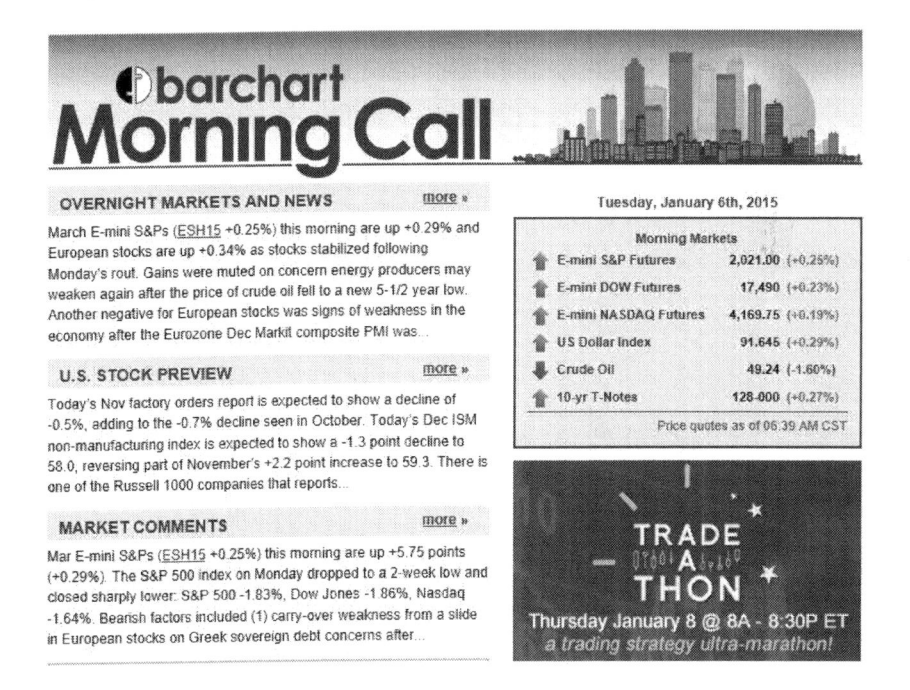

But, we fell behind China for the first time economically as a whole. China has large amounts of gold, and has made energy deals with Russia, whose Ruble is falling, due to falling energy prices.

Interesting political squeeze play by the powers-that-be, who want to prevent the loss of the U.S. dollar as the world's reserve currency (oil is priced in U.S. dollars), and China's attempt to replace it with the Yuan.

These are crazy times, and I could go on and on, but if you've been in the markets, you get my point. Be careful in highly volatile times. Even seasoned day traders stand on the sidelines sometimes. And, it's better to not lose money, than to lose an opportunity.

If you know what you're doing, you can make a lot of money quickly, but you can lose lots of money just as quickly if you don't know what you're doing – be careful – don't lose money.

Ride your winners. Get out of your losers, and <u>don't</u> add to losing positions by "averaging down" and throwing good money after bad. Try to avoid big (10-20% or more) market declines by being invested in "cash," rather than being exposed to the market's decline by being fully invested in stocks.

Get into a true money market or bond fund, not a hedge fund money market or ETF (example etf bond symbols = **TLT, TIP**), with your broker account, even and especially for your retirement account(s). Move your money to protect and to preserve it.

<u>Don't just sit there and do nothing and watch your life savings disappear!</u> **Do something to save it!**

As Warren Buffett once said, the key to successful investing is <u>*"To be FEARFUL when others are GREEDY, and GREEDY when others are FEARFUL."*</u>

There is no better mid and long term measure of economic growth than GDP - <u>Gross Domestic Product</u>. Don't get lost in all of the economic indicators and news reports. Most economists can't even get it right. Let them be confused by it all.

Don't try to predict the economic news or market's directions. <u>Be a trend follower.</u>

"Nobody ever knows what the market will do, but we can <u>react intelligently</u> to what it <u>does</u> do." Benjamin Graham, Warren Buffett's teacher.

Moving Averages are versatile. Use the **10 and 20 "MONTH" Exponential Moving Averages** to gauge mid to longer term *market direction trends and reversals!*

The second to the last time the S&P 500 dipped below the 20 month ema, in a sustained market *down-turn*, was November of 2000. Then it entered a long term decline, and it did not fully recover until it crossed back up and over the 20 month ema in mid 2003.

The last time the S&P 500 dipped below the 20 month ema, in a sustained market *down-turn*, was January of 2008, and it did not turn up until February of 2009!

There have been a handful of slight, short term dips in the markets, below the 20 month ema, since the markets have been *trending up*, providing several trading opportunities. The Dow hit new all-time highs several times last year, hitting 18,046.58 on 12-29-2014 before selling off again. Keep in mind also, that 2015 is the 3rd year for Obama, and the best "presidential year" for returns in the markets, with 2016 being second best. A good tail-wind for sure. Later interest rate increases and lower oil profits are a drag on the economy and markets, however. Pick your hot stocks – watch their charts!

It will be interesting to continue to see how the markets perform regarding the 20 month ema, and our questionable economic future. The charts below end in 2008, and I have not updated them on purpose. Do your homework, and plot your own charts from 2008 to now. *Get in the game.* Have a little fun! Be in the k-NOW!!

Plot the 10 and 20 month exponential moving averages on your charts and see how they "cross-over" one another. The 10 month ema gives you an earlier "signal."

Now change your charts from "monthly" moving averages to "weekly," then to "daily." Can you see how moving averages can help you in both your short, mid, AND long term investing? ("50" and "200" ema's can prove useful to you as well.)

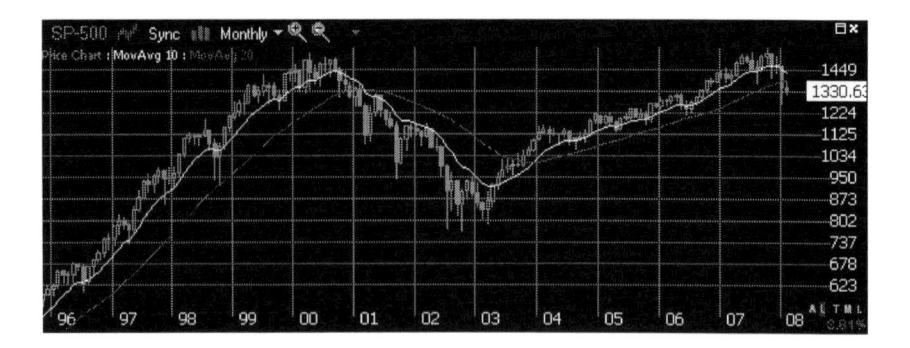

Follow the Dow trends up and down – don't guess - there is simply no need to try to out-guess or predict the markets (unless you can of course).

Consider following and trading the Dow "Diamonds" (DIA), as this ETF closely tracks the Dow Jones Industrial Index. You'll lessen your "watch list" work-load, and you'll be tracking what you can trade directly. Consider also the Dow ETF's from ProShares™.

The S&P 500 closely tracks the Dow. Consider tracking and trading the "SPY" ETF, as well as the S&P 500 ETF's from ProShares (also consider NASDAQ "QQQ" ETF, and NASDAQ ETF's from ProShares).

"Dow Theory" suggests that the "Dow Transportation Index™" (ETF is "IYT") is a leading indicator as compared to the "Dow Industrial Index™."

The "Wilshire 5000" (ETF is "TMW") and "Russell 2000" (ETF is "IWM") indexes may also give you an earlier and broader overall signal of market strength and direction.

You can also trade higher risk "Futures" indexes directly, but this publication is not about riskier futures trading. Also, futures trading is not allowed in your retirement account(s).

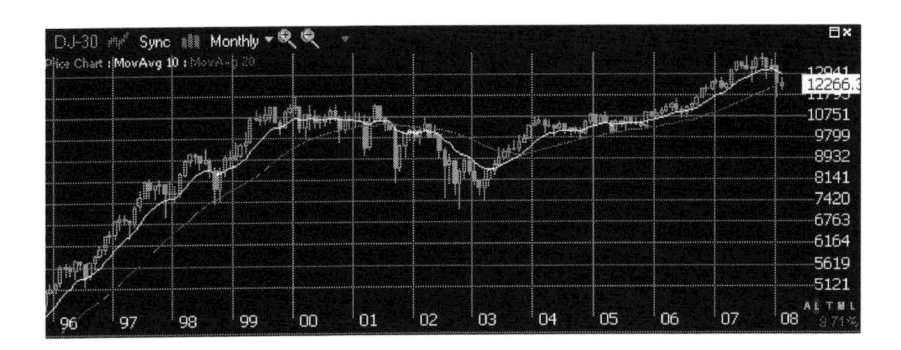

You may be interested in the **McClellan Oscillator**™, if you wish to go a little deeper into tracking trends. It's not found on most platforms, but it is found on MetaStock, TradeStation, and can also be found at <u>www.mcoscillator.com</u> (content by the creators, and a newsletter).

The <u>McClellan Oscillator</u> is an advanced measure of *"advances/declines,"* and <u>assists you with market trend direction</u>.

Another one of my favorite newsletters is <u>Independent Living</u>. Lee Bellinger and Seth Van Brocklin both give you accurate market and investment analysis at a reasonable price. They like to recommend ETF's. This is one of the very best all-around "money" centered newsletters for the average person I've ever read. They can be found at **www.AmericanLanternPress.com**.

I also like Robert Shiller at <u>www.irrationalexuberance.com</u>. He can also be found on **www.amazon.com**. He nailed his predictions of the market's decline in 2000 and 2008. He also has insightful real estate information as well, and he predicted the real estate decline in 2005.

Taxes: Get one or both of the two best books on trading and investing tax strategies available to you. Search for Ted Tesser and/or Robert Green on **www.Amazon.com**.

See your tax accountant or other tax professional.

Most brokers also allow for downloading your investment information to Excel files, and you can use software programs like Intuit's Quicken™ or TurboTax™ ("Premier" and "Home & Business" editions), H & R Block's TaxCut™, and Microsoft's Money Plus Premium™, to capture your trading and investment data easily from these files.

Ken Fisher, of Fisher Investments, says you only need to know 3 general ideas:

1. Invest consistently over the long term, using a winning system and strategy.

2. Overcome obstacles. Be they "personal" or "market" obstacles.

3. Own a "higher knowledge than others" - have an edge over others.

***** **Stick with what is proven to work over the short, mid, and long term - stick with "New 52 Week High" momentum hot stock picks!**

"Sticking to it is the genius."
Thomas Edison.

Free Special Report

Chapter 14: Top 10 Hot Stock And Option Pick Trading Systems And Strategies... *9 Of Which You'll Never Ever Need!*

"Swing Easy - Hit Hard."
Fred Couples, Pro Golfer.

These **Top 10 Hot Stock and Option Pick Systems and Strategies** are <u>NOT</u> old, stale and repetitive newsletter, book, or magazine picks. You don't have to read a stack of books or newsletters written by financial writers and economists, who are filled with theories, what if's, and maybe's.

These top trading and investment systems are simple, proven, successful, and verifiable, and IN ADDITION TO your #1 hot stock pick system – "52 week highs."

I am not a paid affiliate for any of these systems, websites, or products, and I am a paying customer, and I may or may not have positions in the stocks/options/etf's obtained from such services, and these statements are for the sake of complete disclosure and transparency.

The following **Top 10 Successfully Proven Stock Investment & Trading Systems Strategies** are **by and for REAL Investors and Traders**, and they are all immediate and ACTIONABLE systems and picks, with PROVEN track records of SUCCESS! These systems will give you NEW, FRESH, CURRENT, and TIMELY stock and option picks.

The following stock investment systems can also be used for buying options on the hot stock picks. The options systems can also be used to buy stocks. In other words, if you have a good stock pick, it may also be a good option play, and vice versa.

You can use each of these systems as your sole system, or mix and match them for confirmation and higher probability stock and option investment picks.

All of these top and winning systems complement your own new system of picking 52 week high momentum stocks, within the context of this publication.

1. Millionaire traders/investors Chuck Hughes, John Weston, and Ryan Christopher, all use the **New 52-Week High stock pick** concept at the core of their investment system. See Financial Visualizations at www.FinViz.com.

They offer several books on this subject for up to $95, and a $5500 per year newsletter for their top picks, mostly based upon 52 week highs and the use of the 52 week high screen, as well as the **"40 and 80 daily exponential moving average cross-over" system** to signal entries and exits from their trades - both stock and option trade investments. Chuck likes his stock pick prices to start at $75 and run to $100, and if stock prices hit $100, they have a tendency to run to $130. Then he exits his trades at either $100 or $130, depending upon the individual stock's momentum.

Chuck Hughes is so confident in this 52 week high system strategy that he promises an *"investor could make at least $100,000 per year and up!"*

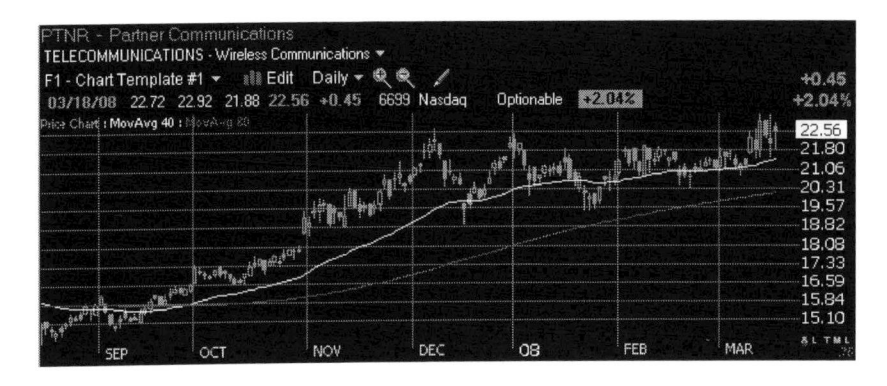

Chuck can be found at www.chuckhughesic.com. Chuck was a World Cup Trading Advisor, and has won several national trading contests.

Chuck is a retired U.S. Air Force fighter pilot, as well as a retired airline pilot. John and Ryan are two of Chuck's successful students.

Chuck and John co-authored **Market Volatility Profit Secrets: How I made more than one million dollars in 26 days, which reveals their 52 week high stock pick, and 40-80 EMA cross-over investment trading system.**

Chuck has over 40,000 customers who have also purchased his **"98.81%"** accurate stock options strategies **"Fail Safe Financial Secret."**

Mr. Hughes says, his *"wealth plan has made him a millionaire and produced over $11 million dollars income in just 4 years, with over $1 million dollars profit through the recent turbulent markets, starting with just $4600."*

Some of his satisfied customers had this to say, *"Thanks to you, I've accumulated more than a million dollars profit over the past twelve months."* and, "I have a $31,513 profit after only 5 days! You have given me the confidence I needed." and, "In less than 6 months, your secret has produced a $671,914 profit. I am in the process of conducting interviews to hire someone to replace me in my real job."

Successful customer results from Chuck's stocks and options strategies include:

* A 74 year old engineer made $92,999 in seven months...with 100% winning trades!
* An Orlando sales manager has hit 100% winners for over $200,000 profit in 14 months.
* A California trader turned his $25,000 into $602,000 in six weeks.
* In Virginia, a man started with just $4,000 and has averaged $1,620 profit per week (an annualized 1935% ROI)!
* A PR rep for a chemical company, has made $66,524 in six months!
* A retired Swiss banker in Zurich, has made $120,265 profit in his first two months!
* A commercial real estate broker, has made $203,944 in six months.

Mr. Hughes can also be reached at; Chuck Hughes, c/o Investment Systems Software, Inc., 217 Paragon Parkway, #306, Clyde, NC 28721.

Ask for current sales literature and **Market Volatility Profit Secrets: How I made more than one million dollars in 26 days.** ($26), and Wealth Building Formula ($95).

He also offers older books titled, The Guaranteed Real Income Program, which involves stock option spread trading and "option writing" for option premium income, and Fail-Safe Financial Program. (Ask for a catalog with current pricing and new offers.)

See also Chuck's other website at **www.chuckhughes.com**.

2. **Investor's Business Daily** at **www.Investors.com**, in my opinion, is the single "must have" investing tool for your premium subscription investing arsenal. In the least case, you should consider the Monday print edition, which comes out on the week-ends, and can be purchased at most book stores and news-stands. IBD gives you reliable top ranking stocks based upon Relative Strength, Earnings, and other proprietary IBD selection criteria.

Their Can Slim™ approach to stock selection is a perennial winner, and can be found as a pre-configured stock screener on **www.tdameritrade.com**, and **www.aaii.com**.

Simply searching IBD's paper for its stock selections is more than sufficient, as IBD has already done the fundamental and technical homework for their stock picks. IBD online is more expensive than the print version, and is not necessary. I much prefer the print edition.

<u>IBD is the single most actionable resource that I've ever seen. If I had one premium resource to choose, it would be IBD.</u>

IBD not only gives you relevant securities data, but they show you what it means and how to use it, and they list top stocks, mutual funds, and ETF's in easy to implement lists.

IBD helps you to lower your investment risks, by selecting top performing stocks, mutual funds, and ETF's for you, with their proven successful proprietary investment methods. How easy is that? Pretty darn easy.

You'll have more hot stock picks than you'll have money to spend on them.

The American Association of Individual Investors, AAII, reported that "stock performance, from 1998 through to 2007, based upon selecting stocks every month by applying IBD's rules for selecting stocks, was the best among well known growth strategies they analyzed, with a cumulative gain of 1522% versus 55% for the S&P 500 during the same period." (IBD's exact figures are 1519.8% v. 54.9% respectively.)

Four of the five top fund managers subscribed to William O'Neil Company's weekly Leaders and Laggards.

Since 1977 this service to top institutional money managers, has averaged 24% per year over the last 30 years, using historically proven investment facts and rules, versus 9.6% per year for the S&P 500.

	O'Neil's CAN SLIM	S&P 500
YTD Return:	46.4%	11.9%
Five Year Return:	9.7%	13.5%
Ten Year Return:	20.1%	5.8%
Inception:	25.3%	4.6%

Data as of 11/28/2014

3. American Association of Individual Investors™ at **www.AAII.com** (only $29/year) offers you 50 pre-configured screens from well known gurus and investment methods, such as Peter Lynch, Warren Buffett, Graham, Zweig, value and growth approaches, Weiss, O'Shaughnessy, IBD Stable 70, etc.

Stock Superstars is a subscription newsletter that gives you their "maximum return at minimum risk" stock picks, at $149 per year, with email buy and sell alerts. 60 well known expert strategies are used to select top stock pick recommendations for you.

Stock Investor Pro ($198 member price; $247 non-member price) is AAII stock screening software that offers you more and current data, as well as more custom screening features.

AAII has many member benefits, including education, local workshops featuring nationally recognized investment experts, model portfolios, various market data, and a yearly Personal Tax & Financial Planning Guide.

AAII's main 50 screens do not include a labeled "52 week high" screen, but O'Neil's Can Slim screen incorporates this concept in its screen – "L" stands for "Leaders."

Stock Investor Pro™ also has the custom capabilities for screening for 52 week highs.

The importance of the guru screens, for those of you who don't already know, is that these methods have worked well in the past for their namesakes, and the men's names labeling these screens have been highly successful money managers, fund managers, and investors. Peter Lynch managed the Fidelity Magellan fund. We all know billionaire investor Warren Buffett.

Benjamin Graham advocates the "value" method of investing, and Warren Buffett is a follower of the Graham/Dodd value method, having learned it personally from Ben Graham.

James O'Shaughnessy manages about $7.2 billion dollars in his O'Shaughnessy Asset Management fund. The O'Shaughnessy screen and investment method is based upon a 52 year study, from 1952 to 2003, based upon data in Standard & Poor's Compustat™ database, and clearly defines the most successful measures in stock investing, and as documented in his book, What Works On Wall Street.

So you see, with their screens on AAII, you get to use "their" billion dollar stock investment screening methods for $29 bucks a year!

These screens, <u>in addition</u> to screening for 52 week highs, are brilliant, smart, inexpensive, quick, easy, and lazy ways to pick your next hot stocks!

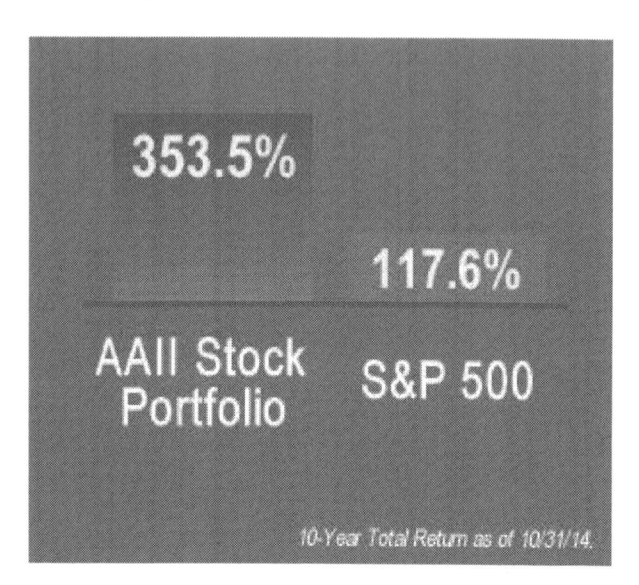

4. Nirvana Systems has **www.OmniTrader.com** ($295 for "end-of-day") and **www.VisualTrader.com** ($295 for "end-of-day"). OmniTrader™ offers you great charts, as well as promotional *PatternTrader™ pattern recognition and buy/sell signals for your own selected stocks, as well as for OmniTrader system selected stocks.

Look for the pre-configured screens that state <u>New 52 Week High</u> and <u>Stocks At or Near 52 Week High</u>, located in the <u>Focus List</u>. As with most software packages, OmniTrader offers many pre-configured stock screens, and you can play with them, but you simply don't need them all.

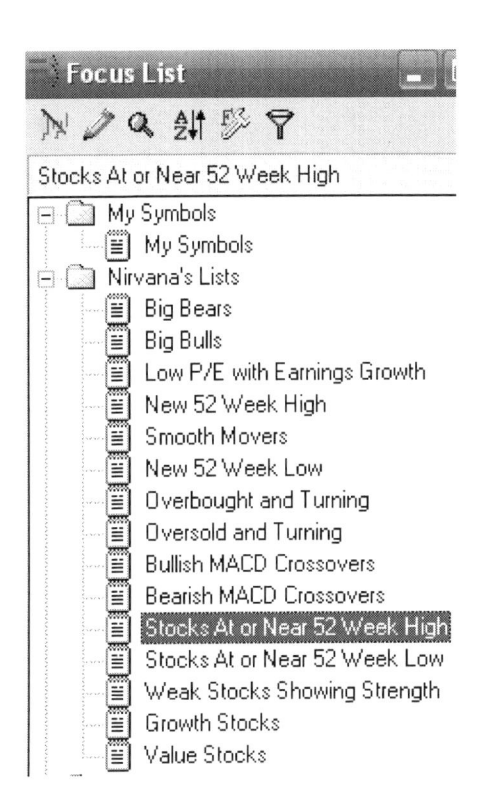

VisualTrader™ is unique in that it offers you visual representations of Industry Sector rotations - which Sectors are currently performing well, and which Sectors are not currently performing well.

Monthly data feed fees are about $29.95, and you can get a discount by making just one yearly payment of $299.50.

OmniTrader also includes dozens of pre-set "systems" and "indicators," in addition to its main "system & pattern signals," to assist you further with your buying and selling decisions, and the additional "systems" also have buy/sell arrow indicators within them. You can mix-and-match your favorites, and "line them all up," to give you more optimum buy and sell signals.

Both OmniTrader and VisualTrader have "real-time" intraday versions as well, for $995 each.

Founder Ed Downs wrote <u>7 Chart Patterns That Consistently Make Money</u>.

*<u>PatternTrader</u> is sometimes offered for $395, with OmniTrader being offered for free, as a "package" purchase. The regular OmniTrader promotions for $295 do not include PatternTrader.

The regular OmniTrader has built in buy/sell "system signals," however. It's worth waiting for the PatternTrader with OmniTrader for free promotional package. They may also offer future promotions with paid OmniTrader plus PatternTrader for free, which would be the same package.

Nirvana also has yearly upgrades for about $149, and also offers occasional product enhancements and add-on modules, which can be viewed online.

OmniTrader Professional™, for $1495, is a high performance "real-time" trading system, with custom programmability, integrated brokerage for trading from your charts, and even total trade automation systems.

Currently, MBTrading and Interactive Brokers offer API access to OmniTrader Pro. You can also choose to trade from your current broker, and simply use OmniTrader Pro for your trading system signals.

Nirvana also offers OmniTrader Remote for remote trading from your PDA or cell phone, as well as Nirvana Club - a community of traders sharing thoughts and ideas about trading and investing.

Enhancements to Nirvana's software also include <u>Power Prospecting</u> and built-in educational seminars. Nirvana is a dynamic company, and is always offering cutting-edge modules for enhanced trading, i.e. Advanced CycleTrader, OptionTrader, Volume System, GMMA, Chart Pattern, Seasonality, and iTLB, etc.

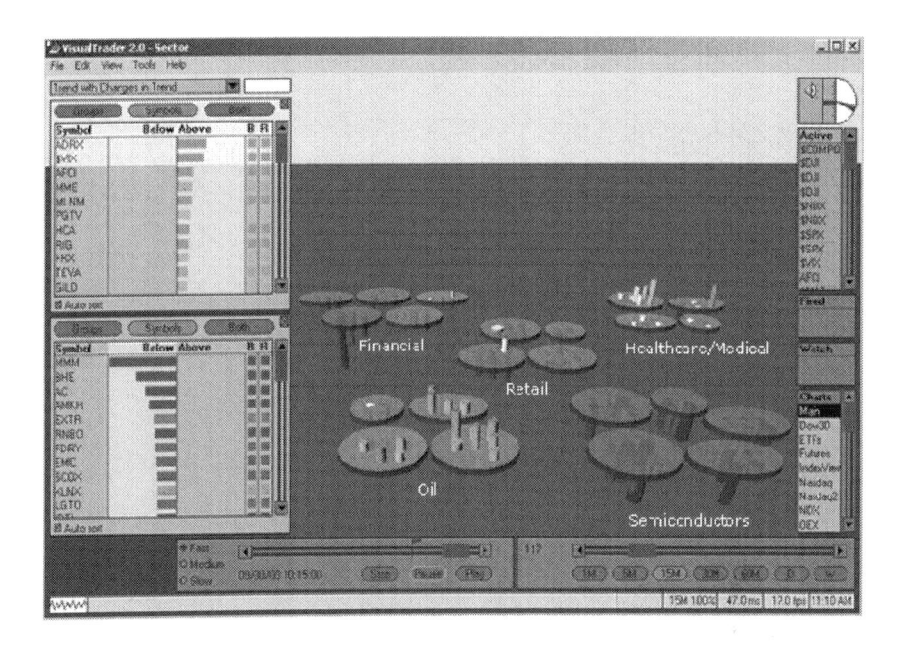

5. www.VectorVest.com VectorVest® boasts up to **99.46% accuracy** in its trading results. It is a proprietary system, and they advertise investment returns of 90% for 2005, 60% for 2006, and 64% for 2007. (Have some fun and see for yourself what it has done from 2008 to 2015.)

$9.95 gets you started on a 5 week trial, and then its $59 per month thereafter, unless you opt for the Express Edition, which is $39 per month.

They have many screens, and all you really need is their top 5 "VST" stock picks, which, not surprisingly, correlates well with its "52 Week High Strategy," "The Best New Highs Strategy," "The Ballistic New High Strategy," and the "High Fliers Strategy" screens.

Their top VST stock picks show up prominently on the first page after login, making it as easy for you as it can possibly get - you don't have to do anything but login! The Express version does this as well, giving you the same VST stock picks.

Their VST picks sometimes correlate well with other 52 week high stock screener picks, but their other VST picks, sometimes can't be confirmed elsewhere, but they do occasionally show up in IBD's Top 100 listings; the variations are due to VectorVest's proprietary stock selection methods.

Dr. Bart DiLiddo, Ph.D., is the founder and developer of VectorVest. Dr. DiLiddo is a mathematician, and since 1978 he began to mathematically define what makes a stock go up or down. He was able to build and create exact equation models that would predictably forecast the rise and fall of a stock's price.

VectorVest screens, ranks, sorts, and analyzes over 15,000 stocks every day, and picks stocks that fit his mathematical models for timing, value, and safety.

VectorVest issues buy, hold, and sell signals, and also ranks industries and sectors.

You also get a free book, with your free trial, titled, Stocks, Strategies & Common Sense, as well as several more free bonuses including, How to Use Options to Supercharge Profits.

His customers state in his ads that:

"I have made $3.5 million shorting stocks; most were chosen on VectorVest. I followed your advice and it paid off. I have done considerable (sic) better than my friends and associates."

"VectorVest is priceless to me for locating the stock with the most potential for safe, vigorous returns."

"Since September 2001, I am pumping gains at an annualized rate of roughly 200% in my margin account and roughly 100% in my IRA. I cannot sing the praises of VectorVest enough. Not only has it allowed me to quit my job as a residential contractor, but it has helped to educate me about the market."

"VectorVest lets me sleep soundly, knowing my nest egg is safe."

"I invested $50,000 on December 1, my return was $30,000 by the end of January 2."

"I subscribe to at least 10 'trading' newsletters and I also use TradeStation, MetaStock and TC2000. VectorVest is absolutely the finest trading software I have ever used. I've been trading stocks and futures for 40 years and developing Windows software for 10 years. I can appreciate the effort that goes into developing and supporting a software package like VectorVest."

"As a seasoned investment professional, I have grown accustomed to using several sources for the purpose of making investment selections and decisions. If I found it necessary to rely on one source, I would choose VectorVest because it combines many of the features (technical and fundamental) that other sources tend to focus on exclusively."

"I recently used parameters which produced over 2,000 choices, made a watch list and refined that to 4 or 5 usable stocks, all in less than 5 minutes...I don't know how anyone can beat that."

VectorVest's Philosophy

Here's how to make good money in stocks at low risk:

- Buy stocks with consistent, predictable earnings growth
- Buy stocks with earnings growth rates of at least equal to the sum of current inflation and interest rates.
- Do Not put more than 10% of your money into any single stock
- Do Not own more than two stocks in the same industry.
- Do Not plunge into the market. Spread the investments over time.
- Use Stop-Sell orders to limit risk

New VectorVest® "Investment Clinics" may be coming soon to your city. Learn about:

1. Buying and selling.

2. Finding the right stocks for you.

3. Cherry picking big winners.

4. Managing your portfolio, and more.

For more information, visit **www.vectorvest.com**.

6. www.ValueLine.com Offers you fundamental data to a greater degree than almost anyone else. That's why Warren Buffett likes Value Line so much. But Mr. Buffett buys entire companies, so he needs the extra data more than the average person.

They have proven proprietary fundamental screens and a "Timeliness" element for picking their hot stocks.

Charts and technical indicators can also be found on their software. $299 gets you a one year subscription to the software and data updates. You can also get a 13 week trial for $75 to check them out.

Most larger libraries have Value Line™ subscriptions for you to read for free.

Value Line states in its sales letters and online, "Suppose you had bought the stocks ranked #1 for Timeliness in April 1965, and updated your holdings once a year, replacing stocks that had fallen in rank with others that had risen to 1 (highest rank)..."

"By December 31, 2007, your portfolio would have appreciated **+24,470%**. That is, your portfolio would have outperformed the Dow, which returned just 1,355%, by **a remarkable 18 to 1** over the same time span. (These results exclude dividends, taxes, and transaction costs. Past performance is no guarantee of future results.)"

But wait, it gets better, even after factoring in 2008-2009....

Further, Value Line states, "Our performance record is discussed here and shown below. The first shows that our 1-ranked stocks had appreciated 49,440%* (before commission costs and before dividends) between April 16, 1965 and December 31, 2013. That compared with a gain of 1,718% for the Dow Jones Industrial Average. That is, if you consistently owned the one hundred stocks ranked number one out of the total of approximately 1,700, the portfolio, as a whole, would have appreciated more than 49,000%. The second graph shows that if you bought all our 1-ranked stocks at year end of each year, held them until the next year end, and then set up a new portfolio of 1-ranked stocks at the end of each subsequent year, the portfolio would have risen 28,586%** since 1965. These are records we believe nobody else has ever matched." (*Allowing for Changes in Rank each week - geometric averaging. **Allowing for Annual Changes in Rank - arithmetic averaging.)

RECORD OF TIMELINESS RANKS

Without Allowing for Changes in Rank

Average Percentage Change in Price
12/31/12 to 12/31/13

Group 1	32.4%
Group 2	35.2%
Group 3	39.5%
Group 4	37.6%
Group 5	45.4%
Average	38.3%
S&P 500	29.6%
Dow Jones Ind'l Avg.	26.5%
Wilshire 5000	31.4%

(arithmetic averaging)

Allowing for Changes in Rank Each Week

Average Percentage Change in Price
12/31/12 to 12/31/13

Group 1	39.9%	45.1%
Group 2	38.3%	43.8%
Group 3	30.9%	35.6%
Group 4	30.6%	36.5%
Group 5	28.2%	34.7%

(geometric averaging) (arithmetic averaging)

RECORD OF TIMELINESS RANKS

Allowing for Changes in Rank Each Quarter

Average Percentage Change in Price
12/31/12 to 12/31/13

Group 1	39.0%
Group 2	38.5%
Group 3	38.9%
Group 4	36.6%
Group 5	37.6%

(arithmetic averaging)

RECORD OF TECHNICAL RANKS

Allowing for Changes in Rank Each Quarter

Average Percentage Change in Price
12/31/12 to 12/31/13

Group 1	42.5%
Group 2	35.8%
Group 3	36.5%
Group 4	43.2%
Group 5	43.7%

(arithmetic averaging)

Source: http://www.valueline.com/About/Ranking_System.aspx

"Hulbert Financial Digest is a publication that tracks the performance of investment newsletters. The Value Line Investment Survey has been at or near the top of their ranking for long-term risk-adjusted performance for much of the past two decades...Beating the market by this much in just one decade is an impressive feat, but doing so for two decades in a row is simply extraordinary, Hulbert wrote."

"Warren Buffett has also praised Value Line: *'I have yet to see a better way - including fooling around on the Internet or anything - that gives me the information as quickly... And I don't know of any system that's as good'.*"

"Using the Value Line system to make sensible investment decisions is easy. *'All you have to do is be able to count from one to five,'* explains Jean B. Buttner, Value Line's CEO."

"You get a full-page report for every one of the approximately 1,700 stocks we follow. Stocks are ranked from 1 to 5 for both Timeliness (probable market performance over the next 6 to 12 months) and Safety."

Preset Screens
- Stocks Ranked 1 (Highest) for Relative Price Performance
- Stocks Ranked 1 (Highest) for Relative Safe
- Stocks Ranked 2 (Above Average) for Relative Price Performance
- Stocks Ranked 2 (Above Average) for Relative Safety
- **Bargain Basement Stocks**
- Best Performing Stocks
- Biggest 'Free Flow' Cash Generator
- High Returns Earned on Total Capital
- Highest Dividend Yielding Non-Utility Stocks
- Highest Dividend Yielding Stocks
- Highest Growth Stocks
- Highest P/Es
- Lowest P/Es
- Stocks with Highest 3- to 5-Year Price Appreciation Potential
- Stocks With Highest Annual Total Returns (Next 3 to 5 Years)
- Stocks With Highest Projected 3- To 5-Year Dividend Yield
- Timely Stocks in Timely Industries
- Untimely Stocks
- Widest Discounts From Book Value
- Worst Performing Stocks

7. Equis (Reuters) offers you **www.MetaStock.com**: $499 end of day, $995 intraday, $59 per month data feed fee, or $595 per year one time payment discount. See their pricing page, as there are *many* other prices and costs to read and understand. MetaStock™ is a perennial Stocks & Commodities magazine "technical analysis" awards winner for software $500 and up. They offer you 21 "add-on plug-ins" for additional technical analysis, including candlesticks, pivots, chart patterns, etc. These add-ons range in price from $299 to $950, in addition to your main MetaStock software program costs.

TeleChart and OmniTrader are also perennial Stocks & Commodities magazine awards winners. I like OmniTrader better than MetaStock, because OmniTrader is simpler to operate, costs far less, and comes with top "patterns and candlesticks" already built in it with PatternTrader™, and without the additional costs of overly expensive "plug-ins."

8. **Oliver Velez's Pristine Method.** The Pristine Method™ of investing is a "Swing Trading" investment style that simply involves the use of Simple Moving Average cross-overs of 20 SMA and 40 SMA, and as applied to the daily, weekly, and monthly charts.

When comparing the daily, weekly, and monthly charts, you are looking for "confluence," or similarity in the Trends of the stock's price direction, be it up or down, and in all three time periods. You want all three time periods to be trending in the same direction, for more accurate and profitable trade investments.

Trade WITH the short, mid, and long term trend lines. Buy and sell using your 20 SMA crossing over your 40 SMA, crossing up to buy, crossing down to sell.

Oliver also discusses buying on "3-5 bar pullbacks," which means; trending stocks will often "pullback," "correct," or decline in price back to the moving average line(s), before returning to its original up-trend and above the moving average line(s).

During these 3 to 5 price bar (or candlesticks) pullbacks, you would "buy" on the pullbacks, and before the stock's price resumes its upward climb and trend.

All broker platforms and charting software programs have *simple moving averages* for you to "plug-n-play."

Pristine, co-founded by Mr. Velez, also offers full trading courses for $95 and up at www.pristine.com, as well as other educational materials, books, dvd's, and software.

The Pristine website is a bit "busy" with lots of offerings; interesting, but not needed.

You can also search his name on **www.amazon.com**.

Look for Swing Trading with Oliver Velez Course Book with DVD, as well as Strategies for Profiting on Every Trade: Simple Lessons for Mastering the Market (Oliver also discusses "candlesticks" in this book), and Option Trading Tactics with Oliver Velez Course Book with DVD, all on Amazon.

Oliver writes, *"Former Wall Street insider, best-selling author, and internationally recognized trader, announces... My system made $86,020.83 in profits... in just one month... using an amazingly simple, easy-to-read trading signal that you can master - in less than a day. These little-known buy and sell signals have helped traders generate profits as high as $15,000 a day - with up to 82% of all trades making money."*

Oliver has been an active trader for over 25 years, and he is the founder and CEO of Velez Capital Management, LLC, which employs approximately 685 professional traders, who have been personally trained by Mr. Velez to trade his own private accounts.

Mr. Velez has appeared on CNBC™, CBS™, Bloomberg™, and FOX News™, and in publications including the New York Times™, Wall Street Journal™, Barron's™, Forbes™, and Stocks & Commodities™ magazine.

Mr. Velez has personally trained more than 60,000 traders, individual investors, and institutional investors.

"Oliver Velez is so confident in his training programs that each student he teaches is **given buying power of $75,000 to $2,000,000 of his own money to trade at no risk to the student!**" *"I just started getting profitable and had a good month in November, making just over $20,000."* Lee S. Visit www.ifundtraders.com.

"All losses are absorbed by Oliver, while he and the trader share in the net profits. Traders who join his elite trading team (approximately 685 total) enjoy some of the best payouts and institutional privileges in the industry."

Visit them to find out if you have what it takes to become a member of one of the fastest growing proprietary trading teams in the United States. **Oliver was the "2009 International Trader of the Year!"** Visit **www.olivervelez.com**.

9. Jon and Pete Najarian use their "Heat Seeker™" technology to follow higher than normal volume and "block" trading activities.

I don't generally recommend newsletters, but these brothers know what they are doing. In fact, Jon was an ex Chicago Bear linebacker (Mike Singletary took his job), who started with about $400, and ran that up to about **$100 million - trading options!**

Jon was also a Chicago floor (pit) trader, who started his own trading company, Mercury Trading, and later sold it to Citadel, one of the largest hedge funds in the world.

Pete also played pro football, and co-hosted CNBC's Fast Money (now off the air).

If you listened to anyone on CNBC, you should have listened to Pete. Jon made an occasional appearance on Fast Money – you should have listened to him too.

Jon also appears on Reuters™, Bloomberg, Dow Jones, Fox News, CBS Radio, CBOE-TV, and appears daily on First Business Television, which is broadcast to about 1.8 million daily viewers in about 200 cities.

They can be found at **www.optionmonster.com** and **www.OptionsHouse.com**.

Jon is also on CBOE-TV™ at www.cboe.com.
Jon, often known after his CBOE floor call letters "DRJ" - has developed and patented trading applications used to identify unusual activity in stock, options, and futures markets, notably the HeatSeeker program, which uncovers extraordinary buying patterns from among the 120,000 quotes per second that stream from America's stock, options, and futures exchanges.

In addition to www.optionmonster.com, Jon's research and analysis is widely cited by leading financial media including the Wall Street Journal, Reuters, Bloomberg, Dow Jones, FOX News Channel, CBS Radio, and CNBC.

He also appears daily on First Business Television, a business news magazine, hosts a CBS Radio show, and web-casts twice daily on CBOE-TV.

Pete is a professional investor, noted media analyst, and cofounder of optionMONSTER™.

After a football career that included several seasons with the NFL's Tampa Bay Buccaneers and Minnesota Vikings, Pete took up trading in 1992 at Mercury Trading.

Two years later, he assumed responsibility for Mercury's risk and arbitrage and later led its entry onto the New York Stock Exchange (NYSE).

He also led Mercury's joint venture with M.J. Meehan, the third largest specialist firm on the NYSE. From 2000 to 2004, he served as president of Mercury, and helped execute its sale to Citadel, one of the world's largest hedge funds.

He is the co-founder of Hedgehog stock, options, and futures trading platform, and together with brother Jon, is a co-developer of the HeatSeeker technology, as well as other complementary programs for tracking unusual buying activity in stocks, options, and futures.

John and Pete have several premium stock-options pick newsletters and personal coaching located at www.optionmonster.com. The higher priced newsletters gets you more data and more picks. Please see their website for more information. They also offer you free options education information.

Jon has a book on www.amazon.com titled, How I Trade Options, and Jon and Pete co-authored How We Trade Options - Building Wealth, Creating Income and Reducing Risk.

Their books are really advertisements for their trading firm www.trademonster.com (now merged with www.OptionsHouse.com), but do contain some useful information.

Jon is considered to be the best options trader of all time by trading insiders!!

Jon expects winning trades 75-85% of the time, and to hold positions about 30-90 days, and earn profits of about 65-75% on each win - often his wins produce far greater returns, sometimes in the triple digits.

Jon spent over 23 years as the "market maker" for over 90 different stocks - trading 30,000 to 45,000 options per day, and over $150 million in stocks each and every day.

10. Dan Zanger's www.ChartPattern.com. Dan is a **CAN SLIM investor** at heart. He calls William O'Neils best seller, **How to Make Money in Stocks**, the "traders bible."

Dan Zanger holds the World Record for boasting a *29,233%* return in his own portfolio in single year. Through his site www.chartpattern.com, Dan runs a newsletter featuring his latest stock picks and analysis that has made some readers over a million dollars.

Dan Zanger has spent close to 20 years and 10,000+ hours studying every type of chart pattern formation imaginable. He combines chart patterns with fast growing companies that boast great earnings and revenue growth. These stocks then go on to yield big returns of sometimes a few hundred percent or more.

Dan holds two world records for the largest portfolio returns in both a 12-month and 18-month time period. He did this during the late 90's, and turned roughly $11,000 into $42 million in about two years.

Dan posts a summary of the overall market and his latest stock picks in his newsletter. Using stock charts, he points out exact buy and sell points, and alerts traders to his trades. Here are some examples of Dan's stock pick successes:

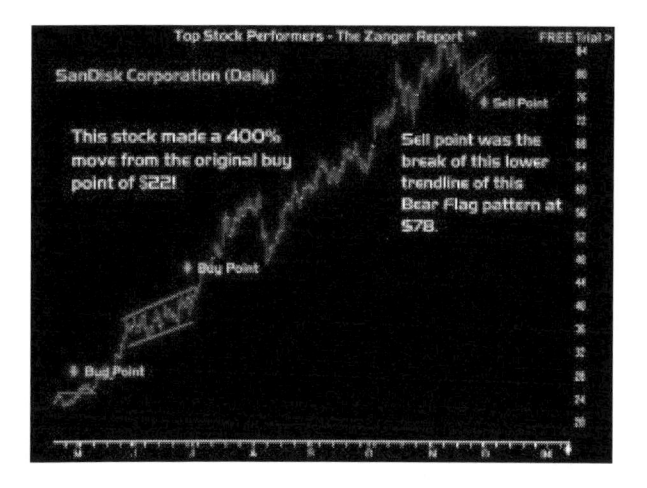

1. Baidu (BIDU) – BIDU was recommended at just over $100 a share. The stock ran up several hundred percent before splitting 1 for 10, and now trades at around $80 or $800 with pre-split pricing, a return of 500+%.

2. First Solar (FSLR) – FSLR was recommended at $31.14. The stock ran up over $110 a share before being marked as a sell, a return of 250+%.

3. SanDisk (SNDK) – SNDK was recommended at $22.00 a share (chart above). The stock ran up to over $80 before being marked as a sell as it broke down, a return of some 400%.

The newsletter is extremely easy to read, and he even has a chatroom setup where you can talk to him live

Here are some customer testimonials:

"Dan, today is my biggest one-day gain – almost 6 figures gain. Thanks for your wisdom. When some people in the chat room today felt the market might sell off after the Fed announcement, but you said judging by the way BIDU was breaking out today, you did not feel the market would sell off. I had a lot of calls of GS, BSC, MA & some stocks such as BIDU, etc. What you said stopped me from selling any before the Fed announcement. What you said came from your many years of experience. Can't find it in any books or from 'financial experts.' You are the best. By the way, I've been to your seminar 3 times & been a subscriber for many years, still learning. Tony."

"Hi Dan, I attended your seminar in May. Since your seminar, I made over $200,000 on your long trades from May through July. Because of the correction, I haven't traded during August, until August 15th, and shorted RIMM and ICE, after your calls, and made $35,000, for two days, during the market steep decline. Thank you for your newsletter, seminar, and your messages in the chatroom. Thank you for being a great trader and not just another guru, whose salesmanship is better than his trading. I have been a successful trader, that has traded for a living for many years, and you have made me a lot better trader. Thank you very much. David Frank."

"Hello Dan, Just wanted to let you know about one of the stories you're responsible for.... My parents are celebrating their 47th Wedding Anniversary today and I had the great pleasure of letting them know that I had surpassed $1,000,000.00 in profits year to date..... I have been reading your newsletter and benefiting from your intra-day information for over a year now.... Priceless, amazing, unbelievable,... I could go on and on.... Just wanted to say thanks for all the dreams you have allowed me to turn into reality... All my thanks, Jeffrey S."

Free   Report

Chapter 15: Bonus Hot Stock Pick Tips!

*"Believe it!
High expectations are the key to everything."*
Sam Walton.

The following stock picking methods are for "less active" investors, and for investors who wish to invest for long term growth and income, and with relative safety. These methods are in addition to your preferred new 52 week high strategy.

1. Additional investment "system" tools for your stock picking reference with fundamental data include:

Standard & Poor's 500 Guide (look for other "niche" S&P guides & books as well, that may interest you); Morningstar Stocks 500; Morningstar ETF's 150; Morningstar Funds 500. Standard & Poor's® and Morningstar® books can be found on www.amazon.com, and at your local Barnes & Noble book stores.

Another surprisingly good book, is the annual The 100 Best Stocks You Can Buy 2015, less than $16.99 currently on Amazon, it is a very good cross-referencing or stand-alone stock picking tool. It can also be purchased at Barnes & Noble.

There are two drawbacks to books (and monthly magazines and newsletters) - timeliness and strategy - they are static picks, and do not change, no matter what the stocks or markets are doing over time, and the picks are not from your own stock picking strategies or software screening efforts.

2. "Dow 30" Investment Facts:

It is possible to construct 5,852,925 "eight-stock" portfolios from just the Dow 30 blue-chip stocks. In times of high risk, or to simply reduce your over-all investment risk over the long term, an additional strategy to consider is investing in "blue-chips," using the "Dogs of the Dow" strategy of rotating, cyclical, winners and losers in the Dow 30.

This strategy may help you to reduce your long term investment risk, and it would also make your stock selection process much easier, simply by reducing your possible stock investment "universe" from over 15,000 securities down to just 30. "Dogs of the Dow" is an www.AAII.com pre-set screen.

Winning with the Dow's Losers: Beat the Market with Underdog Stocks, by Charles Carlson, CFA, can be found at www.horizonpublishing.com and www.amazon.com.
Horizon Publishing also offers you other helpful publications on "DRIP's" and Dow Theory, etc.

3. "DRIP's" are **Dividend Reinvestment Plans**, which allow you to buy stocks directly from certain participating companies, and without paying a brokerage commission (100% commission free).

You can learn more about DRIP's from www.HorizonPublishing.com, as well as from **www.DripInvestor.com**. Drip Investor also offers you a free sample newsletter, a current "Top 10" DRIP's list, and a DRIP's manual with over 1100 listings.

There was an "Annual Standard Deviation" **Risk** of approximately 30% (higher risk) for S&P 500 Non-Dividend paying stocks, versus approximately 18.5% (lower risk) for S&P 500 Dividend paying stocks. The Standard Deviation was measured over a 36 month period ending 6/30/06. Source is EcoWin and Young Research.

Dow Theory Forecasts calculated "relative risk scores" on more than 2600 U.S. traded stocks over a 60 month period, from February 2003 to February 2008. They found that the average relative risk score of the 1338 dividend payers was 65 (higher is better in this example, and represents lower risk), as compared to 34 for the nearly 1300 non-dividend payers. They also found that *dividend paying companies generally are of a higher quality, offer more value and greater financial strength, and are better performers* than non-dividend paying companies.

Since 1926, dividends have contributed 42% of the total return delivered by the S&P 500. A $1000 investment in the S&P 500 in 1926 would be worth $3,313,712 today with dividends reinvested, but only $116,454 without dividends reinvested.

Over the 3 year correction of 2000, 2001, and 2002, the stocks in the S&P 500 that paid dividends actually rose 10.4%, while the non-dividend payers fell -33.19%.

Conventional wisdom says that if you take on more risk, you're repaid with more reward. That's not always true. The NASDAQ, known for its aggressive non-dividend paying technology stocks, actually under-performed dividend paying "utility" stocks over a 30 year span from 1971 to 2001. Even with the NASDAQ's spectacular run in the 1990's, "utilities" still came out on top, and with about half the volatility (only about 10% as volatile as the market generally).

"High-yielding equities are less volatile. Because the companies pay out cash, investors are more willing to hold dividend stocks through bear markets. Hence, they don't fall as far or as quickly as non-dividend stocks." Businessweek™ (2008).

"As a growing number of retiring Americans seek income-generating assets, the importance of personal dividend income will increase." Standard & Poor's.

In other words, <u>Dividend Paying companies may be less risky, and may have the potential to generally out-perform aggressive "growth" stocks, contrary to popular belief.</u>

9 good resources for investing for dividend income and higher yields are:

1. Roger Conrad and David Dittman publish <u>Big Yield Hunting</u> at: **www.bigyieldhunting.com**.

2. <u>Drip Investor</u> at: **www.dripinvestor.com**.

3. <u>Dividend Opportunities</u> at: **www.globaldividends.com**.

4. Morningstar's <u>Dividend Investor</u> at: 1-866-608-9570, and **http://www.morningstar.com/products/Newsletters.html#MDI**.

5. Louis Navellier's <u>Blue Chip Growth Letter</u> at: **www.bluechipgrowth.com**.

6. <u>Money</u> magazine's "Stocks" section lists "Highest Yielding Dow Stocks," as well as "Top-Performing Stocks," "Most Widely Held Stocks," and "S&P 500 Sector Averages."

7. Do a "dividend stocks" search on **www.amazon.com** for the latest, greatest books on dividend investing.

8. Consider also ETF's and Mutual Funds with a "Dividend" focus (VIG, PFM, VYM, DTD, DLN, DTN, SDY, FDL). Check for all current ETF's with companies listed in the ETF section, or through your broker or software platform(s).

9. Also from **www.horizonpublishing.com** is <u>The Little Book of BIG DIVIDENDS</u>, <u>The Best Dividend And Income Investments</u>, and the <u>Directory of Dividend Reinvestment Plans</u>.

Coca-Cola Co.® **(KO)** in their own words, "The Coca-Cola Company has paid a quarterly dividend since 1920 and has increased dividends in each of the last 50 years. The dividend payment amount below is the actual amount paid per common share." http://www.coca-colacompany.com/investors/stock-history/investors-info-dividends.

Gains from dividends and dividend paying stocks currently receive preferential tax treatment. Please refer to your tax resources and tax professionals for more details.

4. If you're a **"one-stop-shopper"** for the long term, and you want the simplest portfolio possible, and with relative safety, consider the following:

A. Invest in the best mutual funds from Fidelity Investments™, Vanguard™, and T. Rowe Price™. See their websites, **www.fidelity.com**, **www.vanguard.com**, **www.troweprice.com**, as well as Fidelity Independent Advisor at: **www.advisor.fidelity.com**, and The Independent Adviser for Vanguard Investors at: **www.adviseronline.com**.

B. Invest in and trade the top performing ETF's from your screening software and IBD.

C. Invest in "Best of Breed" stocks in the top performing Sectors/Industries in IBD.

D. Invest in TDAmeritrade's and Schwab's proprietary retirement funds.

E. Invest in the Dow 30 top performers and highest yielding dividend payers.

F. Invest with your favorite Certified Financial Planner, and in their offered securities.

G. Invest in **"The One Forever Stock,"** Warren Buffett's Berkshire Hathaway™; BRK-A, or BRK-B shares. BRK-A is currently $220,980 as of 1-5-15. In March of 2012, I recommended it at $121,074 per share Class A. BRK-B is currently at $147. I recommended it at $80.71 per share Class B in March of 2012. No stock splits ever. Warren does not believe in stock splits. *"I buy businesses, not stocks, businesses I would be willing to own forever."* Warren Buffett.

There are several premium newsletters that follow Mr. Buffett's stock picks. One is **www.coattailinvestor.com**. **www.cnbc.com** follows Mr. Buffett with free articles. The best free resource is Mr. Buffett's **www.BerkshireHathaway.com**.

H. What stocks are working right now? High flying *New 52 Week High* momentum stocks of course!

5. Last, but certainly not least, Porter Stansberry of **www.stansberryresearch.com,** also supports trading new 52 week highs, as stated, **"New 52-week highs** (as of 12/9/14): ProShares Ultra Nasdaq Biotechnology Fund (BIB), Cempra (CEMP), Dollar General (DG), Express Scripts (ESRX), Fidelity Select Medical Equipment & Systems Fund (FSMEX), ONE Gas (OGS), ProShares Ultra 20+ Year Treasury Fund (UBT), and UIL Holdings (UIL)."

Additionally, Stansberry & Associates Investment Research offers many newsletters, with True Wealth, and True Wealth Systems being two of them. Editor, Dr. Steve Sjuggerud's investment philosophy in *True Wealth* is simple: "Buy assets of great value when no one else wants them... and sell them when others will pay any price." A somewhat contrarian point of view, but still offered here as an investment "style" choice, in keeping with being a "Bonus." They are worthy of your taking a further look at them. It's up to you.

The reason I suggest taking a further look at them is because of their affiliation with Dr. Richard Smith, who also offers his own investment services.

Dr. Smith is a data miner, who was previously employed with top pharmaceutical companies, and since about 2009, has used his data mining skills in stock research with Stansberry Research.

He calls his stock picks "bit stocks." He pays high yearly stock data feed fees to get "bits" of information to formulate his stock picks. His stock picks manifest through the investment newsletter True Wealth Systems. Dr. Sjuggerud edits both True Wealth Systems ($2500/year), and True Wealth ($79/year). Email customer service at **info@stansberrycustomerservice.com** to ask them to get you on their mailing list, and to get sales letters for the above to learn more about them. I'm not affiliated with them, however, I have been a subscriber in the past.

My final point is to re-emphasize Dr. Sjuggerud edits both True Wealth Systems AND True Wealth. I've also noticed similar, *very* similar stock picks are shared between both of these newsletters. See the "Ultra Health Care" pick below. In sum, $79 sounds better than $2500. Many newsletter services offer similar services for a "high" and a "low" price. *Caveat Emptor* my friend. Buyer beware… of the costs of doing business!

Stansberry Research Top 10 Open Recommendations

(Top 10 highest-returning open positions across all Stansberry Research portfolios)
As of 12/09/2014

Stock	Symbol	Buy Date	Return	Publication	Editor
Ultra Health Care	RXL	03/17/11	390.4%	True Wealth	Sjuggerud
Constellation Brands	STZ	06/02/11	340.0%	Extreme Value	Ferris
Ultra Health Care	RXL	01/04/12	329.1%	True Wealth Sys	Sjuggerud
Enterprise	EPD	10/15/08	293.8%	The 12% Letter	Dyson
Altria	MO	11/19/08	266.1%	The 12% Letter	Dyson
Automatic Data Proc	ADP	10/09/08	196.3%	Extreme Value	Ferris
Blackstone Group	BX	11/15/12	173.6%	True Wealth	Sjuggerud
Hershey	HSY	12/06/07	169.9%	SIA	Stansberry
McDonald's	MCD	11/28/06	167.1%	The 12% Letter	Dyson
Berkshire Hathaway	BRK.B	04/01/09	166.9%	Retirement Mill	Eifrig

Please note: Securities appearing in the Top 10 are not necessarily recommended buys at current prices. The list reflects the best-performing positions currently in the model portfolio of any Stansberry Research publication. The buy date reflects when the editor recommended the investment in the listed publication, and the return shows its performance since that date. To learn if a security is still a recommended buy today, you must be a subscriber to that publication and refer to the most recent portfolio.

Each of the above bonus resources offers you an easy and relatively low risk way to create simple stock picking systems for your long term investment portfolio, especially for those of you who wish to be less active investors over the long term, as well as for retirees and wealthy investors, who seek capital preservation and income, especially in "bear" markets.

If you seek even less risk, "guaranteed income for life," annuities can bring you a lifetime of guaranteed retirement income. See your local Certified Financial Planner to invest in annuities for your peace of mind, as well as your freedom from "bear market" crashes and losses of your principal retirement equity. Remember that early withdrawals from annuities can trigger substantial early withdrawal penalties of as much as 15% or more.

Home owners with high equity, may also consider a "reverse mortgage," where you receive guaranteed payments, AND you can live in your home for the rest of your life.

One more chart just for fun…

PAPA JOHN'S INTERNATIONAL INC
(NASDAQ: PZZA)

US Markets Closed
Trade Free for 60 Days

▲ **61.53** +1.02 / +1.69%   After Hours : **61.48** -0.05 -0.09%

Currency In USD. January 8, 2015 4:00 PM EST

Jun 1995   May 1999   Apr 2003   Mar 2007   Feb 2011

Papa John's was starting to break-out to new highs almost 4 years ago, from about $15, rising up to $61.53 today, January 8th, 2015, over 3 times your money back ($46.53), on top of your original investment, or a 322% return on your original investment, if sold today. AND it's STILL reaching new 52 week highs! When will it sell-off? Watch your charts and see for yourself.

This isn't day-trading, and 52 week highs can pay you well over time. The above chart is from **www.MSN.com**, "Money" tab, to "Stock Screener," to "52-week highs."

It simply doesn't get any easier than that shown above.

*"There are no limitations except those you acknowledge.
Whatever you can conceive and believe,
you can achieve."*
Napoleon Hill.

Do You Believe?

"The only man who never makes a mistake is the man who never does anything." Theodore Roosevelt.

"People only see what they are prepared to see." Ralph Waldo Emerson.

"Most people never run far enough on their first wind to find out they've got a second." William James.

"Men occasionally stumble over the truth, but most of them pick themselves up and hurry off as if nothing happened." Winston Churchill.

"Genius is the ability to hold one's vision steady until it becomes a reality." Benjamin Franklin.

"I skate to where the puck is going to be, not where it has been." Wayne Gretzky.

"I never quit trying. I never felt that I didn't have a chance to win." Arnold Palmer.

"How much easier it is to be critical than to be correct." Benjamin Disraeli.

"Great spirits have always encountered violent opposition from mediocre minds." Albert Einstein.

"My brain is the key that sets me free." Harry Houdini.

"To be possessed of a rigorous mind is not enough. The prime requisite is rightly to apply it." Rene Descartes.

"Condemnation without investigation is the height of ignorance." Albert Einstein.

"Fortune favors the bold." Virgil.

"The secret to success in life is for a person to be ready for their opportunity when it comes." Benjamin Disraeli.

**"I have missed more than 9000 shots in my career.
I have lost almost 300 games.
On 26 occasions I have been entrusted to take
the game winning shot, and I missed.
I have failed over and over again in my life.
And that is precisely why I succeed."** Michael Jordan.

Remember this: *Even if web links and economic conditions change, the "new 52 week high" strategy will still work well, it always has, and the "screener" for it will always be found somewhere!*

Isn't it time for <u>YOU</u> to become a

RAGING Bull

?

EXTRA BONUS! Find a $2,000,000 TREASURE CHEST filled with GOLD COINS, GOLD BULLION, and PRECIOUS GEMSTONES! Clues are contained in all of my books for you to find this hidden in plain sight, not buried, modern day $2 MILLION DOLLAR TREASURE CHEST!! It's not yet been found since 2010. In case you missed it, here is the big obvious clue found earlier in this book…

www.collectedworksbookstore.com A good general resource for real gold treasures. Look for **Thrill of the Chase**, and **too far to walk**, by Forrest Fenn, you'll be glad you did.

The gold treasure chest pictured below was purchased for $25,000 all by itself! This is the very treasure chest filled with $2,000,000.00 in gold, coins, and gems!!

Believe it, it's true!

Brian Ault is a successful forex, stocks, ETF, and options trader, who has been trading successfully since 1987. Brian was a stock broker and securities analyst for Fidelity Investments in the 1980's and 1990's. Brian combines his investment and trading knowledge and experience with his highly skilled abilities to research and write about investments and trading. Brian then presents these investment and trading facts in simple to understand layman's terms, making your learning experience fast, easy, and profitable.

Copyright © 2015-2016 by Brian Ault. All Rights Reserved.

Made in the USA
Middletown, DE
10 August 2017